YOU'RE

IN

10 PRACTICAL STEPS
TO INCREASE YOUR ODDS AT
TOP COLLEGES

...THE RIGHT WAY

JONATHAN EVANS &
BHASKAR SAMBASIVAN

ISBN: 978-1-692-17405-7

To all the students helping to build our future...

CONTENTS

ACKNOWLEDGEMENTS

We would like to thank all the students, parents, and admissions counselors whose feedback, both formal and informal, helped shape our book into a truly timely and valuable resource for general audiences. Your comments, questions, and observations were an essential component of our thinking and overall approach to presenting the college admissions process and all it entails in a clear, concise, accessible way.

PREFACE

How This Book Came to Be

"What do colleges want?"

It's a question that can't be answered a single way for every family, or even for a single family. But it's a question that Jonathan Evans answers every single day when working with parents and students as they embark upon their journey to college admission, from selecting courses and extracurriculars in high school to identifying best fit programs at colleges, and from brainstorming topics for application essays to nailing admissions interviews.

One family, the Sambasivans in New Jersey, had come to him with a decidedly typical request: help their son get into the college of his dreams. Their son wasn't on track to be valedictorian and hence wouldn't be among the top 1% of prospective students on paper, but he had a drive and passion that they knew could propel him to success at even the most competitive college. As with many parents starting the college process with their kids for the first time, they firmly believed their child had all the right ingredients to make it into a top school, but the path from hope to concrete reality was not especially clear, and the morass of articles, talks, and discussion forum chatter only obscured things further. After months of discussions with several pricey admissions counseling companies, it became obvious that those options would also not provide their son the boost he needed to maximize his admission odds. Some companies exclusively targeted "test prep," others only provided assistance with application essays, still more offered one-size-fits-all packages – and each one to the tune of thousands of dollars. Thus, the

Sambasivans came to the conclusion that there was not a resource or a company that could comprehensively showcase their son's strengths, address areas for improvement, and match his unique qualities with best-fit schools. Until, that is, they met Jonathan.

From Jonathan's vantage point, the answer was clear within the first hour, as he met their son during an initial consultation and saw how passionately he spoke about technology and business, and especially about studying at a top school in both categories. And as the days gave way to weeks, which gave way to months, Jonathan and the Sambasivans worked meticulously for two years, step by step and side by side along multiple tracks, to maximize his chances at three specially chosen colleges, each with extremely low acceptance rates. Through Jonathan's methodical, deliberate approach, the Sambasivans had finally found the individualized, comprehensive guidance that was missing. Fast-forward to today, and their son is basking in the delight of studying finance and business analytics at one of the nation's top schools, his dream now a reality.

For Jonathan, this experience reinforced the importance of a tailored approach to college admissions. For Bhaskar Sambasivan, this experience, while personally successful, showed that the anxieties that were a recurring theme among almost all parents and students could be addressed through a systematic, step-by-step approach. Then, both Jonathan and Bhaskar came to a mutual realization: *that this system can help everyone.* They envisioned a simple guide of how any family could navigate this complex and tangled web of college advice, selection, and requirements. And so, with that seed of an idea in tow, Bhaskar and Jonathan embarked upon writing exactly that: Bhaskar with his unique lens as a thoughtful and community-minded parent who can give voice to the concerns and unanswered questions of families in similar situations, and Jonathan with his years of expert, insider knowledge and specific, directed guidance of hundreds of families. Together, through this book, they have distilled what every family needs to know to traverse this process, along with a host of invaluable tips and strategies that will make the process not just a successful experience, but a rewarding and memorable adventure they will cherish forever.

FOREWORD

In October of 2018, arguments began in *Students for Fair Admission v. Harvard*, a lawsuit alleging discrimination in Harvard's admissions process, particularly against Asian-Americans. The case provided a trove of insight into Harvard's (until now) less than transparent criteria for admission, chief among them the existence of a "Z-list" by which Harvard admits less academically qualified candidates who have a special relationship with the school (for instance, the child of a generous donor), and a "dean's interest list" that gives preferential treatment to families with social clout. While we don't endorse the use of these special "lists," the case also showed that Harvard takes into account for admission other important factors that do exist within one's control, such as leadership, service, and a whole host of other personal characteristics.

One year later, on October 1, 2019, a federal judge ruled that Harvard's admissions process "passes constitutional muster," and that the school is within its legal rights to include subjective factors in its admissions criteria. Not a terribly unpredictable result, but its most compelling aspect is that it confirms exactly what we've known and shared for years: that Harvard (and hundreds of its fellow undergraduate institutions) utilize a subjective, holistic admissions process that seeks to admit students on the basis of more than just GPA and test scores. And the good news is that most of these elements exist firmly within students' control. Even with the newly unearthed information that the court case has brought to light, however, it is not easy to understand exactly what qualities will most likely propel your child to that fateful day that he or she receives that prized letter of admission.

Given this murky landscape, it is easy to see why so many exceptional students do not get admitted into top schools for which they are eminently qualified. At every turn, whether in one's academic decisions or extracurricular choices, errors both big and small can be the difference between attending one's dream college and settling for a lesser school. We have encountered many students who unfortunately met with this result, either because they did not seek out the necessary information or because they were improperly guided. We constantly hear concerns by parents and students alike – a sense of confusion, of being overwhelmed, of not knowing how to navigate the maze of competing information, information fragmented across dozens of sources in print and on the Internet, and (in some cases) misinformation – and have made it our mission to provide what has been missing: a clear, actionable guide that extracts what is truly needed for aspiring students seeking admission into top colleges and universities.

What our mission is **_not_**, however, is encouraging students to take ethically and legally questionable shortcuts of the sort that have recently dominated the news headlines and gossip magazines. While college admission is indeed a complex process fraught with all manner of stress and confusion, the continued harsh ramifications faced by those involved in the Operation Varsity Blues case demonstrate that unearned short-term gain can quickly turn into long-term pain.

To this end, this book is all about simplifying the overwhelming process of preparing for and completing the college admissions process the right way. From planning the high school academic curriculum to choosing extracurriculars to writing compelling application essays, this book will be a vital companion that will cut through the fog and provide clear, concise guidance from the earliest planning steps to the finish line of being admitted. Our unique perspectives on and insights into the component parts of this process are specifically geared toward clarity and against the mass of confusion and misinformation that you have likely encountered thus far. You can take a deeper dive into each chapter, and periodically give yourself important reminders through the post-chapter recaps that distill the essential information into a helpful bulleted summary.

As the landscape of college admissions continues to evolve, whether as a result of legal developments or otherwise, we will evolve alongside it, continually responding to changes as they emerge and providing the best, most pertinent advice for families. In the end, our goal (and yours) is to ensure that when the time comes for your child to be evaluated by the admissions panel of his or her dream school, you have done everything possible to make their decision an easy "You're in!"

INTRODUCTION

Know What to Expect

Is it ever too late to start planning for college?

This is invariably the first question we get from parents and students. And we invariably respond, "Better late than never!" But honestly, if your goal is to get into a top university, some serious planning and hard work are required.

We have seen some families start counseling and tutoring for their children as early as grade 6. Most families start thinking seriously about colleges when their kids are in their sophomore year at high school, and some at the beginning of the junior year. Every child is different, and so your child's needs will differ based on personality, academic readiness, and a whole host of other factors.

If you are serious about admission into a selective school, the best time to start planning is generally at the end of 8th grade. This will provide adequate time to plan the high school course sequence, extracurricular activities, standardized tests, summer programs, and other activities, and space them out over the next four years. Trying to cram everything in the last year or two will not only exacerbate everyone's stress levels, but also reflect in the grades and test scores produced.

However, if you are reading the book and you are indeed in your junior or sophomore year, there are still many things that you can do to make a significant difference in your application. Planning is key, but when it comes down to it, what matters in the end is the outcome!

What do top colleges look for?

Colleges are vibrant, dynamic environments where students learn from professors, invited speakers, and (of course) their peers. Part of what lends a college campus this uniquely active intellectual flavor is the eagerness that students exhibit in both sharing and taking in new perspectives on topics ranging from the esoteric to the hot button. Ultimately, however, what top colleges look for aren't candidates expert in every single possible area, but students able and willing to be open to perspectives on a global level. After all, their aim is to cultivate students capable of succeeding on the world stage.

As we define it, a "top" college is not necessarily among the top 50 schools as ranked by the various lists you've probably already sifted through. It's the school that is the best fit for your academic, extracurricular, and personal goals, and chances are that it's not a school for which you're already a shoo-in, or the school that all your friends are going to: it's the school that's the best match for you, not for everybody else.

So what is it that a student can do to demonstrate that they are more than willing to fulfill this challenge? You might have created a list of colleges by now, and maybe even determined what your "dream school" is. This book is all about how you can make admission into your dream school a reality, increasing your odds by following our proven methods and strategies crafted from a combination of our professional expertise and discussions with students, parents, admissions and guidance counselors.

In the end, though, it's important to stress that whether or not you ultimately get admitted to your top school, no single school will make or break your college experience. Your four years in college will be marked by amazing insights you'll gain and incredible moments you'll never forget, and as long as you're motivated enough to seek out those things, you'll be able to mold any college you attend into your best fit.

The competitive environment today

Almost every family we encounter echoes the same refrain: "Why is college admission so competitive?" Sifting through a pile of admission statistics, you might feel intimidated by the sharp downward trend in acceptance rates across the board, but you are not alone.

In fact, it's easy to say that many of us would have been rejected by our own alma maters if we were applying today. Standardized test scores have increased, and acceptance rates have sunk. Why has it become so much harder to be admitted?

There are two big reasons: first, there are simply more students. According to the National Center for Education Statistics, the number of high school graduates grew by 20 percent between 2002 and 2013. In 2010, there were 3.2 million high school graduates. This year, the Department of Education estimates that there will be 3.6 million. And the number is projected to increase another 5 percent by 2026. Colleges have simply not kept up with this growth.

Just as importantly, a greater proportion of these students are applying to college. 40 years ago, less than half of high school graduates applied to college, but today, due to a range of social and economic pressures, almost 70 percent of all high school graduates apply to and ultimately enroll in college.

Many students are responding to this elevated level of competition by applying to more and more colleges. In 1990, only 9 percent of students applied to seven or more colleges. However, in 2011, that number skyrocketed to 29 percent.

And in the past few years, many seniors have gone even further to guarantee receiving an acceptance letter. A 2015 Washington Post article reported that students in a New Jersey-based charter school applied to more than 45 colleges on average. One student even applied to more than 70 schools!

Another major cause for this new frontier of competition is rise of online applications. Almost every college now offers online applications; at most schools, it is the only method for applying. The number of students applying online jumped from 41,000 in 2000 to more than 800,000 in 2015.

The introduction of one-stop portals like the Common Application makes it even easier to apply to more colleges. More than 700 colleges nationwide are part of the Common Application network. While application requirements can vary, most colleges require a single essay (which students can re-use for all of their chosen schools) and the submission of a few biographical and demographic details. With a few clicks and the virtual swipe of a credit card, students can spontaneously apply to more and more colleges. And they have. In 2018, approximately one million students used the Common App, doubling the number from less than ten years prior in 2008.

Among the top tier of public and private liberal arts institutions, applications have increased by one-third or more during the last five years alone, due in large part to the rise in international student applications. Yet, the available spaces have remained relatively constant.

To be fair, the frenzied college admissions panic is really only a factor among the country's most elite schools; we're talking about just 50-100 schools, when there are 4,000 or so colleges and universities across the country. Nationally, the acceptance rate for undergraduates is actually a comforting 70 percent.

Among more selective schools, though, the numbers reflect just how much more competitive the college admissions has become. This past cycle, Princeton University rejected almost 96 percent of its applicants, a large percentage of whom boasted perfect SAT or ACT scores. It's obviously not enough to be a strong student with great test scores. For instance, a perfect score of 800 on the SAT Math Subject Test Level 2 would only place you at the 81st percentile of the overall population of test-takers nationwide. So while objective characteristics will get you considered, it is the softer, subjective items that make a difference at the end.

Consider the following graphs (courtesy of Cappex). The x-axis represents the spread of standardized tests scores for both SAT and ACT, while the y-axis indicates GPA. The star represents where a student who had applied to a highly selective school stood in comparison to other applicants. A quick glance at the first graph might lift your spirits immeasurably, while the second might have you throwing in the towel before you've even started. As you can see, this student was no sure bet to get in: his chances, as dictated by the pure numbers, were 50-50. In the end, this student was accepted into this college. So why was he admitted, while no shortage of candidates with higher test scores and higher GPAs were not? It's important to understand the decision making process at colleges.

5

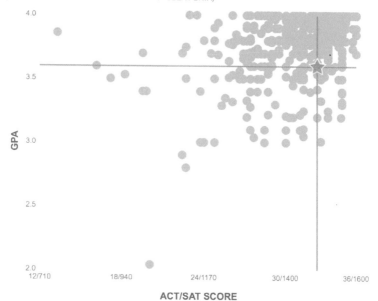

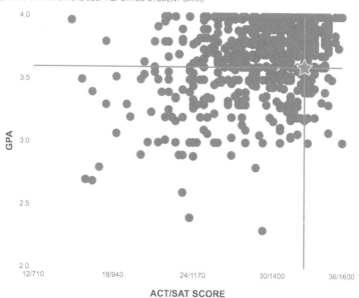

The holistic admissions process

In most Western countries, college admission is a pure numbers game. For an American student to be admitted into top British universities such as Cambridge University or Oxford University, for example, comes down mainly to their performance on standardized tests like the SAT and International Baccalaureate program. Even in the United States, at some universities (especially large public universities), admission staff are practically forced to admit "by the numbers." With swelling applicant pools, time to individually review each prospective student is limited. Certain state-required policies or standards may also be at play.

On the other hand, when it comes to the most selective colleges, grades and test scores only scratch the surface. The pool of applicants is so wide and so deep that grades and test scores merely open the door.

At moderately selective schools as well, scores are only a part of the holistic review. More qualitative measures of an applicant's fit take on added importance. Essays and recommendations are more likely to be read and considered carefully, the personal interview may carry more weight, and the entire application is considered from the perspective of whether the student will be a good fit for the college and whether the college can best fulfill the student's needs and interests.

We're sure you have heard examples from your neighbors and friends that "so and so is shocked that he didn't get into this college even with a straight 4.0 GPA." In a holistic review, there is no formula or guarantee that a student will get into their desired college just because they have scored "A" in all their subjects. This is where most parents and students might lose the plot: they will spend too much time honing their grades, but not spend enough time planning and shaping the application for the holistic admission review process.

The holistic admission review is looking for students who stand out, have differentiated themselves, who have gone above and beyond, have done something unique, or who have excelled in a particular field, and not necessarily the student with the best grades.

The rest of this book will shed more light on the holistic admission process, what colleges look for, and how to prepare for and shape the application in the best possible manner. We have organized this advice, which has helped hundreds of determined and creative students realize their full potential, into Ten Steps capturing the entirety of the admissions process.

Planning for success

For most families, planning for college naturally involves following some, if not all, of the steps that the rest of this book will cover. However, that planning is often done in a reactive manner that lacks deliberate intent. Our goal is to help provide a sense of structure to make this planning as productive as possible.

To that end, we provide specific tips and insights drawn from our years of experience working with students who have successfully implemented these approaches to maximize the benefit of each of the ten steps. These concrete, actionable tips numbering in the dozens throughout this book will serve as a crucial guide to not only keep you on track as you navigate the admissions process, but also to ensure that you dramatically differentiate yourself for the admissions committee that will ultimately evaluate your application.

You may have already made some progress on some of the Ten Steps, but the embedded tips we provide for each will almost certainly change the way you think about approaching the entire admissions process. For example, while you may have already done college visits, have you truly demonstrated interest in a way that will leave an impression on those schools?

And so, here is our first tip, which you should keep in mind as you continue reading through the book:

☞ *TIP 1: Be prepared to challenge what you thought you knew about the college admissions process.*

Building the Ten Step Plan

STEP ONE

Be Clear About What Your Passions Are

MYTH: "I participate in a varsity sport, do community service, and play violin, so I'm a sure bet for colleges."

This is a common refrain among many students who believe that their extracurricular activities will definitely propel them into the top tier of candidates at their choice schools. What they may not realize, however, is that their interests may not necessarily come across to colleges as genuine passions, but rather as mere interests that do not carry the depth or longevity that colleges value.

☞ *TIP 2: Distinguish between passions and interests*

As we define it, interests are hobbies that a student values, but which are not essential to capturing their level of responsibility, diligence, and persistence as other commitments. Think after school chess club or intramural field hockey.

A passion, on the other hand, reflects a deeper engagement with a narrower range of commitments across an extended, multi-year period that has demonstrated growth over the course of that period rather than exhibiting a flat, constant level of engagement over the entire duration. This might look like a progression from Junior Varsity soccer, to a spot on the Varsity team, to a prized slot on a club team. That is, a clear evolution in rigor and level of competition.

For instance, we spoke recently with a student who was unsure about whether or not his lifelong engagement with playing guitar constituted an interest or a passion. We simply asked him, "Do you see yourself devoting your life to playing guitar professionally?" to which he replied, "It's probably more of a hobby." If you can envision yourself honing a skill and turning it into a career, chances are that it is something that you can indeed call a passion, but otherwise, both for college admissions and for your life path more generally, it's an interest.

Once you've confirmed that a particular endeavor is a passion for you, the next step is to find ways to stand out from the crowd in that field. In today's competitive environment, almost every aspiring student is involved in a number of activities and is able to demonstrate excellence in many of these as part of the application process. So the question becomes: what's the differentiating factor that makes the student stand out?

☞ TIP 3: Find multiple roads to showing your passion

While colleges appreciate students having several interests, they look for demonstrated passion in one or two areas and the concrete achievements a student has made in those areas. For example, a student might join the robotics club at school and participate in it for all four years of high school – a strong, elevated level of interest. If they wanted to clearly show passion for robotics, however, they could go above and beyond what their school offered, meaning participating in independently organized competitions, engaging and connecting with individuals and entities specializing in the field, attending a summer program to enhance knowledge of this discipline, and more. It does not matter whether they won every tournament or landed the best internship, but finding multiple avenues to demonstrate that they are passionate about a particular subject will communicate to colleges that they are serious about learning as much as they can about the subject, and thus help their application shine.

The key is for students to gain experience that will help colleges understand that they have not only put a great deal of thought into their future academic and professional aspirations, but also acted upon opportunities to put that interest into practice. For a student who is interested in practicing medicine, for example, the best avenues to demonstrate potential for success in this field include volunteering as a junior EMT or shadowing a local medical practice. A student who plans to pursue the humanities, on the other hand, should submit literary pieces to competitions like the Scholastic Art & Writing Awards to gain practical experience in and national recognition for their craft.

☞ *TIP 4: Keep an open eye and ear to identify passion*

While developing passion is important, it's not easy for children (especially at younger ages) to know what they are passionate about. This is where parents can play a key role in helping them think through what their interests are by talking to them and sharing their experiences. Parents can also be on the lookout for indicators that signal their child's potential for success. Perhaps you've noticed that your child exhibits a high degree of ease with numbers and might be suited to a career in mathematics, or maybe your child is a gifted listener who could excel as a counselor. By identifying these indicators early on, you can help focus your child's effort and time on a few things as opposed to getting involved in everything. In other words, sometimes less is more. This is why planning your interests is key.

☞ *TIP 5: Colleges don't play favorites, and neither should you*

There is no one activity that colleges think is inherently better than any other particular activity. They look at activities as a whole and the overall narrative a student's activities produce rather than the area of interest their activity happens to fall under. They don't like athletes more than they like musicians. In fact, college welcome diversity, and want to admit students with a wide range of interests and backgrounds.

☞ *TIP 6: Find activities that help exhibit leadership*

While it is indeed the case that colleges do not give certain types of passions preferential treatment, one of the most important things that colleges look for is leadership. Leadership can take multiple forms, but the glue that holds them all together is that you're taking initiative and making something happen. Whether it's being Student Council President, captain of the baseball team, or even starting a business, the bottom line is that when a student is coming up with ideas and trying to have an impact on the world around them, that's leadership.

Leadership is an attribute that evidences itself in the way that a student acts and in the results that they produce. Ultimately, what a student should want to show a college is that they have had an impact on their school and community at large, and so it's helpful to tie their passion to something that allows them to make that impact in the first place.

☞ *TIP 7: Don't stick with a passion that isn't working out...*

Colleges want to see evidence of consistent excellence. What does excellence look like, exactly? Maybe a student is a gifted violinist, and maybe plays with their local orchestra or youth symphony. Or maybe they're really good at rhythmic gymnastics or fencing. Whether through traditional extracurricular activities like sports or music, or through something more original, you need to forge a path to that "excellence" door, whether doing something that thousands of others do, or something less common, like being an amazing sitar player. Whatever that thing is, if a student can do it with excellence and find ways to stand out, colleges will notice.

If, however, that excellence is hard to come by, or that activity simply does not gel well with a student, there is no shame in moving on and finding something new. The time spent on an unproductive endeavor cannot be reclaimed, so the longer you spend extracting droplets from a cactus, the less time you will have to delight in the oasis just ahead.

☞ *TIP 8: ...but don't be a dabbler either*

While exploration is key, colleges do care about commitment. They want to see activities that students have shown they have spent a lot of time doing. It's crucial to show passion in a narrative that's extended over the course of multiple years. Academics come first, but students need to find ways to maximize their time committed to activities that demonstrate their passion. That might mean ramping up summer activities or taking on activities that are more self-directed in nature (writing articles, submitting art to competitions, and the like),

17

but regardless, students need to show colleges that they are willing to dedicate the time to cultivate their passions in meaningful ways. This means that while students should indeed explore multiple interests on their pathway to discovering their passion, even including some failed ventures, they should also stick to what they ultimately do land on and not be a dabbler.

☞ *TIP 9: Make them say "Wow!"*

Admissions committees are made up of human beings, and like all humans, react strongly to novelty. When novelty is presented the right way, that first impression can be your biggest asset. What is the "wow" factor, and how you do get it? Well, you get it by doing something that makes people go "wow!" Part of the prerequisite of being a "wow" activity is the idea that you're doing something that not every high school student is doing. Whether that's qualifying for the top levels of a particular endeavor (sports, music, etc.), you can also come up with a "wow" factor in unconventional ways.

Maybe the activity you're doing is not the most usual, but you rise to the top of it. There was a student we had worked with several years ago who got into MIT, and she was creating MATLAB coding and studying epidemiology using raw data from Twitter, and number crunching to see if she could read trends in influenza throughout different regions of the United States. She was able to showcase a self-study project that most high school students would not have ever thought to do, and because of that, she was able to show that she could do the high level research required, and without any help.

☞ *TIP 10: Find ready-made pathways for your passion*

Since "wow" is not always easy to come by, however, it is also important to explore traditional routes to demonstrating passion. Depending on your academic interests, there are a few avenues you should definitely pursue. For instance, if you plan to study English or become a literature major, you should submit your original writing to the Scholastic Art & Writing Awards, which confer nationally-recognized honors each year on the basis of student creativity.

Similarly, if you are passionate about mathematics, excelling as part of your school's Math Olympiad team or competing in the annual American Mathematics Competitions (AMC 8/10/12) will demonstrate your aptitude for the subject, while also potentially granting you honors that will help you stand out among your peers.

STEP ONE RECAP:

Planning is key to discovering the passions that will help you stand out in college admissions.

Colleges want to see that your passion has given you opportunities to demonstrate leadership, continued excellence, and long-term commitment.

Your academic interests should help inform which opportunities you explore, so research programs that will enable you to showcase your passion most effectively.

STEP TWO

Research Colleges for Your Best Fit

MYTH: "My grades and test scores make me a shoo-in at my preferred college."

Choosing a college is a decision that shouldn't be taken lightly. Many high school students get wrapped up in big name colleges, schools that older friends or siblings have attended, or colleges that their parents hope they'll attend. These are valid reasons for considering a college, but they aren't the best way to choose your college.

Instead, you should take a more holistic approach to choosing colleges. To do this, you'll need to research colleges carefully using a number of different resources. Once you have an extensive list of colleges that meet your search criteria, you'll need to narrow them down according to your own priorities.

☞ *TIP 11: Go deeper than the standard "Top 50" rankings for your best-fit school*

There are over 5,000 colleges and universities in the United States. Among them, there are a select few that consistently dominate annual lists of "top" colleges and thus dominate the conversations that you have with friends and the list of schools to visit, to the exclusion of the vast majority of other schools. The problem is that these lists are based on a combination of factors that may or may not have any specific relevance to your academic aims, even as they influence your conscious or subconscious decision making.

The fact is, you are unique. No one before or after you will ever be the same exact kind of community member, student, or athlete that you are. No one will bring with them the exact same strengths and weaknesses or preferences and dislikes. This means that your search for a college that fits you best will also be unique. While it's helpful to use popular rankings like those released by the U.S. News and World Report or Forbes to learn about schools that might interest you, ultimately, there should be a lot more behind your search for the best college for you.

For example, suppose you are an extremely well qualified student interested in attaining an undergraduate business degree. You might use these rankings as your initial guide as to where to apply, and be enticed by schools at the very top, whose positions would seem to signal they are the best fit for you and the estimable academic credentials you bring to the table. However, what this surface-level treatment fails to consider is that one must go past the top five to even land on a school that offers an undergraduate business program. Therefore, you should focus on the rankings for specific disciplines, since the top-ranked schools in a general sense might not represent the "top" schools for your area of interest. In the event that you overly prioritize general rankings over a more specific deep dive into specific areas of study, you might do yourself and your college selection a terrible disservice.

As you begin researching colleges, then, it's important to recognize what a "good fit" college looks like for you and you alone, and what factors will help you make that determination.

☞ *TIP 12: Be realistic in how you segment your schools*

Are your grades and test scores in line with those of admitted students? Do you have a reasonable chance of getting into the college? Beyond that, will you be able to keep up with the level of academics expected of students there? These are important questions to ask as you decide whether a school is a good fit academically.

There are resources you can take advantage of to compare yourself directly to other students with similar academic credentials who were admitted to or rejected from your choice colleges. Chances are that your school already makes these resources available through portals such as Naviance, which provided the following graphs showing how a particular student fared against the previous year's graduating class for a particular school.

On these graphs, a student's GPA is plotted on the y-axis, while standardized test scores on ACT and SAT respectively are plotted on the x-axis. The included key indicates students who were admitted, rejected, or were given some other decision. For a student outside the box formed by the dashed lines, the combination of GPA and standardized test scores signals a higher chance of getting into a school, while students within the box would stand a lesser chance of admission.

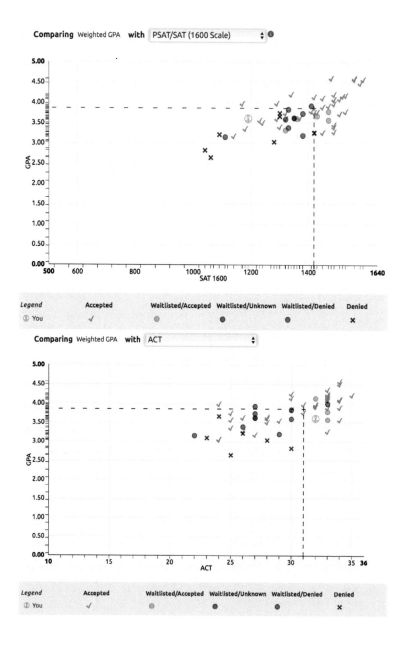

Comparing Weighted GPA **with** PSAT/SAT (1600 Scale)

GPA
SAT 1600

Legend	Accepted	Waitlisted/Accepted	Waitlisted/Unknown	Waitlisted/Denied	Denied
You	✓	●	●	●	✕

Comparing Weighted GPA **with** ACT

GPA
ACT

Legend	Accepted	Waitlisted/Accepted	Waitlisted/Unknown	Waitlisted/Denied	Denied
You	✓	●	●	●	✕

While you should always take into account that college admission's is indeed a holistic process, having a GPA or standardized test scores in SAT or ACT that are not in the ballpark of previously admitted students is a major roadblock that might, from a practical perspective, help you rule out certain schools that are simply not realistic targets worth spending your time and money pursuing. At the same time, though, you might also be inspired to try a test again. Unlike the grades on a transcript, standardized tests allow you to "rewrite" history, so to speak, and present a totally different, and more favorable image, than your current crop of scores projects.

Regardless of your placement on graphs such as these, you should divide your list of schools across three separate categories: "Safety" (which refers to schools at which your grades and test scores exceed the 75th percentiles of admitted students), "Target" (which refers to schools at which your grades and test scores situate you among the students historically admitted into the school), and "Reach" (which refers to schools for which your grades and test scores are below the median statistics of admitted students, or schools whose acceptance rates are so low – typically under 20% – that even the most well-qualified candidates cannot be guaranteed admission). You might want to consider a general rule of thumb to be having three to five schools in each category, but this number can vary for each student.

You should also be mindful of the fact that different academic programs within a university may have varying levels of selectivity. For example, while NYU's acceptance rate across all undergraduate programs was 28% in 2017, its undergraduate business school Stern admitted only 11% of students that same year.

Categorizing schools is a crucial element in helping focus your college list, and so you should make sure to do it early.

25

☞ *TIP 13: Take advantage of zero-effort admissions boosts*

There are ways you can get a leg up to go beyond what the on paper statistics might convey. Within certain academic programs, for instance, demographics can give you a boost. Engineering programs tend to favor female applicants, who are underrepresented in the discipline, while elementary education programs might offer preferential treatment to male applicants, whose presence is similarly lacking in this field.

You can also gain an advantage by attending a public college in your state, since they tend to favor in-state residents. And for students applying in-state to a private college, while you won't get that same boost as your public school counterparts, you won't be evaluated less favorably than out of state students (contrary to popular opinion!).

☞ *TIP 14: Consider costs, but don't let sticker shock rule a school out*

Finances are a substantial factor in many family's college decisions. You'll need to have a conversation with your parents about the colleges you can afford. You'll also need to weigh the scholarships and aid packages that are offered at each college before you can make an informed decision.

Later in the book, you will find an addendum that delves more deeply into how to pursue financial aid and help fund college through private scholarships and other means.

☞ *TIP 15: Consider intangible factors to narrow down your selection*

Some students have particular needs that need to be met on

campus. Others prefer access to certain campus resources. If you know that an extensive research library or a community of diverse students are important to you, you will need to find out if these are available at the schools you're interested in attending.

Ultimately the school you attend will need to prepare you for your future. Does it offer the majors you're interested in? Does it offer combined lines of study or other specifics you're interested in? Start with your long term goals and work backwards from there to decide which programs are most important to you in choosing a college.

While talking with friends and family shouldn't be the backbone of your college research, it should still play an important role. After all, your friends and family know you best and may have valuable insights into colleges that will be a good fit for you. Also, attending a college where you know a few people might be an important factor in your college search. Only you can decide how important it is to attend a school where you already know some students. Just be wary of weighing your friends' college choices as heavily as more important factors like programs of study and quality educational resources.

☞ *TIP 16: Make your guidance counselor your best friend*

One valuable resource is your guidance counselor. Optimize conversation about college choices with your guidance counselor by preparing for it ahead of time. Make a list of your priorities in a "best fit" college. What is its ideal setting, geographical location, size, and specialty? Consider things like selectivity, demographics, and campus culture as well.

Once you have developed a list of your own priorities, share it via e-mail with your guidance counselor. Ask if he or she has some time to sit down with you to discuss your priorities and offer some insights into schools that he or she feels may be a good fit.

Many guidance counselors juggle the needs and questions of hundreds of students, but if you prepare for your meeting in advance and give your guidance counselor the information he or she needs to prepare as well, you can expect to have a much more productive meeting.

Counselors can also give you a heads-up when college fairs are being planned. College fairs are another way to learn more about colleges. Essentially, these are events where college admissions representatives get together to present information about their colleges and to attract students who might be a good fit. Remember, it's not just students who want to find a college that fits—colleges want to attract students who are a good fit as well!

☞ *TIP 17: Find your "just right" size*

The size of a campus can definitely affect your college experience. A big campus can be exciting, but also overwhelming. And a small college can provide comfort, but also be isolating. It's important to figure out what your preferred college size is.

Colleges considered "small" typically have fewer than 5,000 undergraduates. Private colleges like Colgate make up most of this category, but there are small public colleges too, such as Delaware State University. "Medium" colleges have between 5,000 and 15,000 undergraduates, and include universities like Brown, Duke, and Yale. On a "large" campus, you would find more than 15,000 undergraduates, and have a campus size to match.

The following is a table of campus sizes for a sampling of schools to provide an illustration of the various possibilities you can choose among:

Campus Size by Total Undergraduate Enrollment (2018-2019)		
Small	Medium	Large
Amherst College: 1,836 Babson College: 2,342 MIT: 4,547	Princeton University: 5,394 Carnegie Mellon University: 6,655 University of Pennsylvania: 10,033	Rutgers University, New Brunswick: 35,641 Arizona State University, Tempe: 42,427 Texas A&M University, College Station: 53,065

Deciding among college sizes often comes down to the social environment you prefer. Knowing whether you feel more comfortable as "a small fish in a big pond" or a "big fish in a small pond" can help you make a decision. Smaller schools can easily set the stage for camaraderie and team spirit. You can get to know just about everybody in a small school, and see familiar faces whether you are in the library, the cafeteria, the quad, or in class. Larger colleges may seem impersonal on the surface, but most offer many opportunities to become part of a smaller community of students with common interests. You may need a bit of self-control to say "no" to all the socializing that tempts you away from your studies.

Small colleges are more likely to offer classes with fewer students, enabling professors to give students more individual attention. At larger colleges, classes may be more lecture-oriented. But many such classes are supported by lively discussion sessions. Also, university honors programs can provide a small-class environment. Therefore, small classes aren't the exclusive domain of small colleges.

In the end, your campus experience is what you make of it, and regardless of campus size, you will be responsible for charting your own path. However, you will make the most of your four years on campus in an environment where you are comfortable, so make sure (through research, including campus visits) to figure out where your preference lies.

☞ *TIP 18: Choose your "home away from home" wisely*

As much as academic performance or athletic offerings, a successful college experience can boil down to quality of life. Choosing a college can mean choosing between plush dorms or tiny bunkers, a lively social scene or quiet boredom, gourmet meals or a mess hall. Your college will be your home for four years, so it's important that you consider factors beyond academics. You wouldn't purchase a home after merely checking out the house itself: you would research the neighborhood's schools, walkability, and other factors that might affect how much you can enjoy your new abode. So why treat college any differently?

One student we encountered, for example, was in the process of completing a transfer application because she had failed to take into account her desire for proximity to a vibrant urban center, which her original school did not offer. A more deliberate approach to ensuring your happiness on a campus can help you avoid future headaches. Whether it's proximity to a bustling metropolis, reliably sunny weather, or an active athletic culture, there are certain qualities that will make life both on and off campus a more memorable, exciting experience, and you want to figure out what those traits are. Otherwise, the highlight of your four years of college might sadly be the day you finally leave. At the same time, though, it's important to keep things in perspective.

If you truly can't imagine being on a campus without a healthy political culture or a lively city center nearby, then quality of life factors can be the make-or-break that helps guide your decision-making, but they're not the end-all, be-all. Unless, of course, you have arrived at the stage where you are splitting hairs between a couple agonizingly close college choices. In that instance, a less than ideal meal selection or one too many rainy days can help tip the scales in favor of one over the other.

☞ *TIP 19: Have an organized approach*

As you go about determining your list of colleges, you will want to add them to a college application spreadsheet. At this point, you may have some idea of whether or not you are willing to make an early decision commitment to a particular school, or you might be deciding between multiple schools. In any case, you can add the relevant application deadlines that reflect your current preferences, and then make changes as you finalize your list.

School	Common App?	Sent ACT	Sent SAT	Deadline	Word Limit	Prompt	Done (Y/N)	Notes
Boston University	Y							
Carnegie Mellon University	Y				.			
Duke University	Y							
Georgia Institute of Technology	Y							
Johns Hopkins University	Y							
Northeastern University	Y							
Northwestern University	Y							
New York University	Y							
Princeton University	Y							
Rice University	Y							
University of Michigan	Y							
University of Notre Dame	Y							
University of Pennsylvania	Y							
University of Texas-Austin	N							
University of Virginia	Y							
Villanova University	Y							

STEP TWO RECAP:

Begin identifying colleges that are a good fit by researching academic programs of interest and by utilizing resources that let you compare your academic record to past admittees.

Divide your range of college choices into "Safety," "Target," and "Reach" categories.

Choosing a college involves a range of factors, including academics, selectivity, and cost, along with quality of life factors like geography, so consider all of these elements before making your ultimate decision.

Your academic interests should help inform which opportunities you explore, so research programs that will enable you to showcase your passion most effectively.

STEP THREE

Make the Most of
Your Academic Record

MYTH: "Colleges favor students who take many AP classes."

Your grades throughout high school are the most important factor in college admissions. While colleges also carefully consider your standardized test scores, essays, recommendation letters, and other personal factors, they view your grades as the most reliable predictor of your academic success in college. So where do grades fit in your overall admissions process?

☞ *TIP 20: Take control of your grades when you have the chance*

Admissions officers consistently say that your day-in-day-out grades are the best predictor of your academic performance in college. Research shows a strong correlation between high school grades and not only academic performance in college, but retention and graduation rates as well.

While standardized test scores still play an important role, admissions staff recognize that your one-day test score may be impacted by a variety of factors such as test anxiety, inadequate sleep, lack of exposure to test-taking strategies, and test center distractions. But your grades show whether you have demonstrated persistence and focus on academic performance throughout your high school years. Even if you haven't been able to demonstrate your best academic performance until now, however, it's never too late. Maximizing your grades in the final stretch is not ideal, but it communicates to colleges that you are serious about putting the work in to show your academic prowess. You can't go back in time and change your old grades, but you still have control over what you can do now.

☞ *TIP 21: Create a positive academic trajectory*

The trend in your grades is extremely important. Often students take time to adjust to the greater freedom and responsibility of high school, and this is reflected in weaker grades during freshman year. Some colleges, such as Stanford University, explicitly state that they do not place importance on freshman year grades. "We will focus our evaluation on your coursework and performance in 10th, 11th and 12th grades, primarily in the core academic subjects of English, mathematics, science, foreign language and history/social studies."

All colleges place more emphasis on your grades in junior and senior year. Some don't even consider freshman year grades. Some colleges that do not consider freshman year grades: include Carnegie Mellon, Stanford, Princeton, and all of the state universities in California (UCLA, UCSD and others).

Therefore, even if your freshman year grades were not stellar across the board, an upward trajectory in your grades in the following three years will provide a boost, showing colleges that you were not only able to bounce back from a disappointing start, but to do so as the rigor of your curriculum increased exponentially. On the other hand, while colleges will not be able to evaluate your full senior year grades prior to admission, they do require your final report card for senior year, so a precipitous drop in performance can prompt them rescind their acceptance offers.

In addition, if you are applying to a specialized field, your grades in certain courses will receive more attention. For example, for business or engineering programs, your math grades are particularly important. For pre-med, your science grades will be looked at closely.

☞ *TIP 22: Show academic rigor*

The strength of your curriculum plays an equally important role. Rigorous courses include accelerated, honors, AP (Advanced Placement), IB (International Baccalaureate), and dual-enrollment courses (in which you receive college credit as well). Colleges encourage students to take on the most challenging curriculum that they can reasonably handle. Williams College, for instance, advises, "Applicants to Williams should pursue the strongest program of study offered by their secondary schools."

Students who are particularly ambitious would be well advised to take rigorous classes beyond the curricula of their high school. These are offered at local colleges and universities or via online schools. One example of a such a rigorous course is multivariable calculus, which follows AP Calculus BC in a formal math sequence, but is almost never offered in high school. Therefore, for a prospective math major, a class like this can elevate one's math bona fides quite dramatically. Likewise, students seeking advanced study in areas like art can take specialized art classes in their community if their high school does not make those readily available.

Students might also consider doubling up on rigorous courses offered by their school in their primary area of interest if their academic schedules don't permit taking these classes in separate years. Students interested in social science might take both variations of AP Government (Comparative and United States), while a student interested in natural science might take both AP Biology and AP Environmental Science.

☞ *TIP 23: Plan ahead for a balanced course load*

It's important that you develop a preliminary plan of courses when you begin high school as a freshman. You can then re-evaluate your plan each year, based on your academic performance, your interests, your college goals, and your commitments to extracurricular activities. Your coursework should be your top priority in high school, and at the same time try to live a balanced life with sufficient time for activities, family, friends, and sleep!

There are many ways that you can reach your potential with your academic performance. Most importantly, engage in your courses. Keep up with homework, try to review your notes regularly, and don't wait until the last minute to study for tests or write your papers. If you need help, see your teacher, work with other students, and use review books.

☞ *TIP 24: Understand your transcript, and how admissions evaluates it*

Admissions staff always view your transcript within the context of your high school. Colleges recognize that schools vary greatly. As Northwestern states, "Every secondary school is different in its level of competitiveness and in the range of courses offered. These factors are also considered when admission decisions are rendered."

In addition to evaluating your school's transcript, colleges typically recalculate your GPA using a standard formula that converts the weighted GPA to an unweighted GPA, so that they can compare students from different schools with different GPA scales. Usually, colleges will use a 4.0 scale, where A+/A = 4.0, A- = 3.7, B+ = 3.3, B = 3.0, B- = 2.7, C+ = 2.3, C = 2.0, and so on. Beyond this generic unweighted scale, however, most colleges keep track of the number of AP and Honors classes a student has taken each year to determine if the student has adequately challenged himself or herself. Therefore, while most colleges have their own specific methods of normalizing GPA, the holistic approach extends to this area as well.

Sample GPA Conversion Table

Multiply the number of credits for each class by the corresponding numeric grade. The total points then gets divided by the number of classes you have taken. Here's an example of how a weighted GPA of 3.93 on a 5 point scale gets converted to unweighted GPA of 3.47 on a 4 point scale.

- "CP" represents an entry-level course
- "Honors" represents the next level up in the course
- "AP" represents the highest level of achievement in the course through College Board's Advanced Placement program

Subject	Letter Grades	# of Credits	Weighted GPA	Total Weighted credits	Unweighted GPA	Total Unweighted credits
CP English	B+	5	3.33	16.65	3.3	16.5
AP Physics	B-	7	3.67	25.69	2.7	18.9
CP Calculus	A	5	4	20	4	20
Honors Government	B+	5	4	20	3.3	16.5
Honors French	A-	5	4.33	21.65	3.7	18.5
CP Computer Science	A+	5	4.33	21.65	4	20
Photography	A	1.25	4	5	4	5
Total		33.25	**3.93**	130.64	**3.47**	115.4

☞ *TIP 25: Develop the habits of "A" students*

The first habit that you should pick up for that "A" grade is to study everywhere and anywhere. If you've got ten extra minutes, and you're waiting for mom to pick you up, then get out some vocabulary flashcards and use that ten minutes. You can even get an app on your phone to study vocabulary. If you're brushing your teeth, tape all of your Spanish words to the mirror so that you can study for the quiz while you brush your teeth. You can also get audiobooks, a great "hack" in terms of studying everywhere. You can listen to *The Scarlet Letter* while you're at cross-country practice. If you want to get the best grades you can, being able to maximize your time and study in every little nook and cranny that you have, even while you're doing something else, will benefit you.

Second, it's essential to prioritize. There's a myth that people who always get "A"s always do all the homework early and perfectly, but that's impossible. However, what you can do is figure out the most important assignment that's due and what subjects you most need that "A" in. If you already have a 97% in Algebra 2, you're not going to be studying for that final for very long, especially if you've got an 89.9% in English class, because that's a make or break exam. Also, know how much things are worth. If one assignment is a journal entry and isn't worth much, don't stay up all night working on it when you know you need the sleep for your Biology AP exam tomorrow. You need to spend time on things that are worth your time.

Third, you should seek out any and all opportunities to improve your grade through extra credit. Your teacher won't always give you extra credit, but it is a nice conversation starter. You can just ask your teacher, but the bottom line is that the worst answer you'll hear is no. This goes for individual assignments as well. If you get a bad grade, ask if you can re-do it or re-submit it, or do a second assignment as a makeup.

Fourth, you need to familiarize yourself with your teacher's expectations. A common question is, "How in the world do I figure out what my teacher wants?" First, if you study past assignments and quizzes, you're going to be able to review those and see what you got marked down for, and why points were taken away. Was it grammar, was it ideas? Another source that you can use to be more aware of your teachers' expectations is study guides. That's usually a pretty good indication of what will be on a test. You have to figure out what your teachers' expectations are, and embrace them.

Finally, and not so surprisingly, you need to maintain a good image. You have to make the most of every opportunity that you can so that when you really have the time to dedicate to a project, you've gone above and beyond what you need to do. You're categorized by your teacher as a "good" student or a "bad" student, and when you've been put in the former, you're going to be judged according to a halo effect that you will radiate. Even if you have no time to do your assignments, scribble something down over your lunch break. Figure out a way to write a paper on the bus. It's not ideal, but it's better to do something than nothing. You need to create the image that you're an overachiever, so that even in those times when you're forced to be imperfect, you can still save face and be credible.

STEP THREE RECAP:

Your grades are the most important factor in college admissions, but the rigor of your curriculum and the overall trend of your grades are also key.

When building your course schedule, you should prioritize enrolling in classes that are most closely related to your primary academic areas of interest.

Maintaining a strong academic record is about more than just studying hard, as the habits of "A" students will help you study smart.

STEP FOUR

Make Your Standardized Tests Stand Out

MYTH: "SAT is better than ACT (or vice versa)."

There are almost 2,500 accredited, non-profit four-year colleges and universities in the United States. Their admission requirements have never been identical, and in recent years the criteria have only intensified. Unsurprisingly, then, the role that standardized tests play in admissions decisions has evolved.

☞ *TIP 26: Understand why standardized tests exist*

Performance in a rigorous high school curriculum is the best predictor of performance in college and is the most heavily weighted factor at almost all selective colleges. However, two flaws make GPA imperfect as the sole criterion for admission. First, course difficulty and grading policies vary from teacher to teacher, school to school, and state to state. Second, grade inflation has compressed the GPA scale. As more students earn A's, it becomes harder to distinguish among applicants.

The proper role of standardized tests is to complement the use of GPA and other factors in the admission process. The SAT and ACT address the two primary problems with grades. They provide a common baseline for all students, and they are designed to provide a useful and consistent distribution of scores.

☞ *TIP 27: Recognize the differences between SAT and ACT*

The tests share quite a few traits, not the least of which is their focus on passage-based questions in their respective reading sections and on Algebra 1 and Geometry in Math. However, there are some major differences as well. The ACT's English section is mainly grammar-focused, so there is quite a bit of memorization needed for concepts like punctuation, subject-verb agreement, and the like. On the SAT Writing, however, there is a much greater emphasis on rhetoric questions. In the context of SAT, rhetoric refers to the use of language to express ideas clearly and directly, and includes question types such as redundancy, transitions, and paragraph development.

Furthermore, ACT tends to be preferable for students strong in the computational aspects of math because it permits calculator usage for the entirety of the Math section (rather than just half), and because the reading comprehension considerations are minimized (i.e. no open-end---ed grid-in questions). The ACT also includes a Science section that tests students' ability to interpret data of a wide variety of presentations, such as research summaries and data representation in the form of tables and charts. Each test's optional essay also differs, with the SAT offering a rhetorical analysis task, while the ACT includes a persuasive essay. Finally, the ACT provides significantly less time per question, which makes it even more important to consistently apply approaches for time management, such as effective annotation and process of elimination.

For SAT, a strong background in literature is essential for excelling in the passage-based questions, which lean more heavily on writings from the 17th and 18th centuries. ACT, on the other hand, is more about effectively identifying question type, such as main idea, details, and inference, to glean meaning from pieces that are generally simpler, but which allot less time to comprehend them. When it comes to math, the best test-taking strategy for SAT is to underline key parts of the question before attempting any computation, since (especially for the non-calculator section) the difficulty of these questions emanates from the often deliberately vague wording they employ. ACT, however, is much more focused on computation (and omits a formulas reference sheet), so being familiar with how to apply the formulas you have learned and use a calculator to cut down on the manual work of the section is key.

☞ *TIP 28: Take the right test for you, at the right time*

The ACT is accepted as an equal to the SAT and has, in fact, been the more popular of the two tests since 2010, and by a growing margin. A generation ago, however, most high school students took the SAT or ACT with little or no awareness of the other test, despite the fact that colleges have long accepted the SAT and ACT interchangeably. Today's widespread acceptance of both tests and an array of additional testing-related options have allowed students greater choice but have also caused confusion for families not accustomed to the decisions involved.

The exact test dates will vary from year to year, but the annual testing calendar is consistent. Keep in mind that you can take tests more than once, an option that many students elect.

Please see the following table outlining the test dates for SAT, ACT, SAT Subject Tests, and PSAT, and AP Tests:

	SAT	ACT	Subject Tests	Other
September				
October				**PSAT/NMSQT**
November				
December				
January				
February				
March				
April				
May				**AP**
June				
July				
August				

There is no "best" time to take the SAT or ACT, as each student's readiness level and preparation strategy will differ. Generally, though, it is advisable to take the test after completing a full sequence of Algebra 1, Geometry, and Algebra 2, which would usually be concluded by the beginning of junior year. Since college application deadlines for seniors can sometimes fall early in the school year, it is also best to make sure that any retakes are completed with ample time to submit to colleges.

☞ *TIP 29: Don't discount the significance of PSAT*

In addition to the SAT, The College Board administers the PSAT. Unlike the SAT, you do not register for a particular test date, since there is one national test date in October. The PSAT does not play a role in college admissions, but exceptionally strong performance can qualify students for scholarship funds through the National Merit Scholarship program overseen by The College Board. Each state has its own cut-off score, with some as high as 1480 out of a maximum possible 1520 points, so it can take a nearly perfect performance to qualify.

If you prepare for the test and perform extremely well, the scholarship funds are a great bonus, but the true benefit in terms of admissions is that you will have earned a national level honor that few students can make claim to.

☞ *TIP 30: Choose subject tests for depth and breadth*

Some schools require or highly recommend SAT Subject Tests, which are subject-specific, 60-minute tests covering math (Level 1/2), science (biology, chemistry, and physics), social sciences (United States and World History), humanities (literature), and foreign language (including Spanish, French, Mandarin Chinese, and others). These tests are rigorously evaluated at the most competitive schools, and can help demonstrate a student's mastery of a specific content area.

However, subject tests are also important in helping demonstrate that a student is able to excel in a wide variety of disciplines. For example, a student interested in STEM should absolutely take subject tests as required in their field of expertise, such as math or biology, but would also benefit from doing well on a test like Italian, which they might not need to spend too much time preparing for if they have already done well in that class in school.

You should confirm each school's individual policy with regard to subject tests.

☞ *TIP 31: Consider an independent study in AP*

As noted earlier, AP courses are a great way to demonstrate to colleges that you value a rigorous educational experience and are willing to go above and beyond to challenge yourself in the classroom. However, not all schools offer AP's, and schools that do might not offer the one you're most interested in pursuing. This is especially applicable for AP tests in foreign languages for which a school does not provide instruction, or for specialized disciplines like Music Theory or Art History.

Luckily, the lack of an AP class in your school's curriculum does not mean that you cannot register for and take the AP exam itself. The only difference is that the class will not appear on your transcript the same way it would for students who take the AP as both a graded course and a standardized test.

There are reasons why a student might pursue an independent study in an AP class even if their school offers the course, though. Sometimes students load up on so many AP classes that they leave themselves little room to actually study for the AP exams administered in May. The value of an AP class, beyond its elevated academic rigor, is that it is weighted in a way that dramatically increases a student's GPA, but all those gains can be wiped away with a poor result on the course's associated standardized test. Teachers are responsible for assigning a student's score in the class, but have no role in grading the actual test.

Therefore, while it is advisable to take as many AP's as a student's schedule permits, it is also important to note the danger of scoring very well in the class based on one's transcript, but turning in a poor performance come test day. A 1 or 2 out of 5 might not only put that strong grade under some unwanted scrutiny, but make colleges question the credibility of your transcript as a whole. This does not mean that you should shy away from taking an AP class: it simply means that you must take the test as seriously as you take the letter on your transcript. And if you're not confident that you can get a great score on the AP test itself, taking it as an independent study will at least allow you to withhold your score, consequence-free.

☞ *TIP 32: Don't settle for "just enough" practice*

Because standardized tests like AP, SAT, and ACT present questions in unique ways, you have to match your content knowledge with an equally strong familiarity with the strategy involved to do well. This means taking official practice tests so that you can become intimately acquainted with the ways that the questions are worded, the best way to pace yourself within a section, among other considerations.

Even for students whose practice has produced multiple perfect scores, there is no point at which they should rest on their laurels and think that they have done enough work to tide them over through test day. Consistent success on standardized tests requires a persistent exposure to the material over an extended period of time rather than in punctuated spikes of activity.

Since College Board and ACT only offer a limited number of official practice tests, though, you should consult with your guidance counselor or tutor to procure additional tests. Practice makes perfect, but even practice takes some advanced planning!

☞ *TIP 33: Ready your body and your mind for the test*

When preparing for the SAT or ACT, the psychological factors can be just as instrumental as how well you've mastered the content and strategy of each test. For example, if your preparation was limited to the same environment, whether your room or one library you kept returning to, you might unwittingly find yourself growing overly accustomed to a familiar set of surroundings. Once you're plucked from those comfortable trappings, though, and are in a new testing center on the day of the real thing, you might wind up frazzled in a way that you could've avoided by varying the environments in which you had been preparing earlier on.

Your mental attitude can be important in other ways, too. Taking any test as impactful on your future as SAT or ACT comes with an automatic helping of nerves and stress, but you want to be able to overcome it and clear your mind so that you can perform at your best. After all, you've already prepared as best as you possibly could, so you have every reason to walk into the test center with a more "zen," relaxed mindset rather than as a tense ball of nerves. It'll certainly reflect in your score!

☞ *TIP 34: Understand the curve and plan accordingly*

Students are often surprised to learn that even after they have determined which test is best suited for them, that particular test has different variations that might have dramatic implications on their score. This is because for both SAT and ACT, each individual test date has a unique curve that is predetermined by the test makers. In some instances, this means that they deliberately administer an "easier" test that has a harsher curve, while in others, a more "difficult" test would result in a more generous curve.

Because of the curve, while your score from a given test date might be satisfactory, an equal performance on a subsequent test date might actually produce a substantially better score. On the June 2018 SAT, for instance, three errors in the math section resulted in a score of 720 out of a maximum possible 800 points, while the very next test date in August had a much more generous curve, assigning a score of 780 to that exact same number of errors. While there is no way of knowing beforehand which test dates might produce a harsh or lenient curve, whether you're pleased with your score or not, a retake might make a big difference in improving your score, even in the absence of a dramatic improvement in actual performance.

☞ *TIP 35: Take advantage of superscoring*

Hundreds of schools superscore both SAT and ACT, which means that colleges will only consider your highest scores on individual sections of each test, across multiple test dates. This makes it even more advantageous to take the SAT or ACT more than once, since a weak performance on one section can be overcome with focused practice, even if the other sections on which you originally scored very well see a worse performance the next time around.

Superscoring can even figure into your test preparation strategy. Suppose, for instance, that you were unable to adequately devote enough time to all of the sections of a given test. You could use your limited time to zero in on one or two particular sections that are of the most pressing concern, and then take the test again with a greater focus on the areas that you could not fully address the first time – without colleges taking into consideration any of your weaker scores.

There are some schools (and it is a good idea to check a

college's website to get the most up-to-date superscore policies) such as the University of California system and University of Texas Austin, that do not utilize superscoring. As such, it is ideal to cover all the sections of a test fully prior to an initial attempt, but in the event that it is simply not feasible for any reason, superscoring at least helps minimize the impact of such limitations.

☞ *TIP 36: Be ready for Round 2 or 3, but don't overdo it*

While the curve and the option of superscoring can be a strong motivation for a retake, students might have a host of reasons to take a standardized test like SAT or ACT again. Maybe they were feeling unwell the first time, or were distracted because of some unfamiliar sensory distraction they had not adequately taken into account, or even just blanked out due to an unfortunate bout of nerves. It can also be the case that a student might want to reconsider which test is best for them. This vast spectrum of possibilities raises the question, of course, of how much sense it makes to take a test multiple times, and if so, how many attempts are ideal.

The answer can vary for each student, especially given that for many, the first attempt might be taken "cold" without any directed preparation. Even with a solid first outing, though, it makes sense to take SAT or ACT more than once. After all, because it's a standardized test, all the work you put in the first time should give you more solid footing the next time around. The general rule of thumb, then, is to plan to take the test at least twice.

At the same time, though, you shouldn't use the option of multiple sittings as an excuse to slack off: your score won't magically increase just because you happened to take the test already. It is generally advisable to sit for no more than three attempts: one as a first earnest attempt after diligent preparation, another as a measure to ensure you've left no stone unturned regarding the curve or other factors that might have impacted your score, and a third if necessary to maximize your score, particularly if you are targeting the superscore option presented by each test for a specific section. After a certain point, though, you run into diminishing returns territory, and are likely better off using your limited time in other ways.

Another factor comes into play here, as well. Some schools also require you to submit your entire history of scores across both SAT and ACT, so sitting in for a test just for the sake of it (and ending up with a poor score on your record) might end up working against you later on down the line.

☞ *TIP 37: Don't "rush" to report your scores unless it's a must*

When you register for a test, you have the option to have your scores sent to up to four colleges free of charge. However, you should not elect this option unless you are a senior hoping to have your scores "rush" reported for schools that have November deadlines for early decision or early action that will need your scores as soon as possible if you've taken the November test date for SAT, for instance. If you send the scores later, the first four schools will still be included free of charge.

Since you can send your scores to schools prior to the application deadlines, you should submit with ample time to spare since some schools require not just the application by their stated deadlines, but test scores as well, and unlike the instant submission that you're granted for the application, standardized test scores have a turnaround time of up to 5 business days without rush reporting. Of course, as you submit SAT, ACT, and subject test scores, you can fill out your college application spreadsheet appropriately.

School	Common App?	Sent ACT	Sent SAT	Deadline	Word Limit	Prompt	Done (Y/N)	Notes
Boston University	Y	X	X					
Carnegie Mellon University	Y	X	X					
Duke University	Y	X	X					
Georgia Institute of Technology	Y	X	X					
Johns Hopkins University	Y	X	X					
Northeastern University	Y	X	X					
Northwestern University	Y	X	X					
New York University	Y	X	X					
Princeton University	Y	X	X					
Rice University	Y	X	X					
University of Michigan	Y	X	X					
University of Notre Dame	Y	X	X					
University of Pennsylvania	Y	X	X					
University of Texas-Austin	N	X	X					
University of Virginia	Y	X	X					
Villanova University	Y	X	X					

☞ *TIP 38: Be choosy with your scores*

You should think strategically about which scores to send to colleges. Most colleges accept both SAT and ACT, and so it's in your best interests to submit the test that better reflects your strengths. You also have the option to submit your subject tests using Score Choice, which means that even if you took multiple subject tests in one sitting (as you can take up to three at a time), you only should submit the ones that you want colleges to consider. Some colleges specifically request that you submit your entire history of standardized test scores regardless of your performance, so for these schools, you must submit everything, including original scores if you retook a test multiple times.

In some situations, a student might have taken SAT or ACT as early as middle school for any number of gifted and talented programs that require standardized tests for admission. It goes without saying that a student in this position need not submit their scores for those particular sittings, since most students taking these tests before high school are not doing so for the purpose of college admission. After high school, however, it would not be advisable to take

SAT or ACT on a whim.

☞ *TIP 39: Take advantage of colleges' flexible testing requirements*

Ironically, the trend at selective universities has been toward more flexible testing requirements, even as the competition to gain admission increases. Fewer colleges require SAT Subject Tests, the essay component of the SAT or ACT, or (with test-optional admissions) any sort of standardized tests at all. Students therefore have the opportunity to apply to many colleges without providing standardized test scores. This option is not offered by many of the most competitive institutions, but for the ones that do, it represents a powerful alternate pathway for students who stand to benefit from it.

STEP FOUR RECAP:

There is no best time to take standardized tests like the SAT/ACT or subject tests, but you should plan them around your exposure to academic concepts.

You can take standardized tests multiple times, so you should think strategically when it comes to submitting test scores, including using superscore.

Because each college has its own specific standardized testing requirements, it is important to research exactly which scores you need to submit to a particular school.

STEP FIVE

Don't Just Visit, Demonstrate College Interest

MYTH: "Visiting a college is enough to show that I'm interested in it."

Almost all colleges have a record of your college visits and any sessions or events that you may have attended at the college. While it is fine to apply for a college without visiting, it does raise a question of how serious and keen the student is about this college and on what basis their interest for the school might have formed. While most colleges do not explicitly state that they would expect students to demonstrate interest in the college, admission evaluation committees in some selective colleges look for this demonstrated interest. Here are some ways you can demonstrate this interest over and above simply attending an information session or campus tour.

☞ TIP 40: *Have a clear plan pre-visit*

Before you visit, you should have a clear plan for what you hope to see. In most cases, a visit will be in the form of a guided tour or on-campus information session, but with proper planning, you will be able to schedule a one-on-one meeting with an admissions officer. These meetings, which most often take the form of informative interviews, can help establish positive relationships with the people who might be the ones making that admissions decision in the near future.

If you are especially organized, you can even identify a professor or department head specializing in your preferred area of study using the college's website, and reach out to schedule a face-to-face meeting. Such a meeting would not only serve as a valuable resource as you learn more about your area of study, but also potentially create a relationship that will serve you well in the years to come at that school.

☞ *TIP 41: Be observant and take copious notes*

Beyond actively seeking out resources that can help you gain keen insight into a school's unique qualities, you can also gain strong insight into the school by simply being observant. Take copious notes, and keep them in a place you can easily retrieve them from later. Unless you are capable of committing everything to memory, you should start the habit of taking notes either on a small notepad or notes app on your phone to capture information that can prove very useful later.

Once the time comes to apply to the school, your visit will provide a crucial basis of knowledge that you will be able to drawn from in your supplementary, school-specific essays. By using your notes and follow-up experiences as material in your writing, you will immediately stand out compared to the much larger cohort of applicants whose essays are unable to achieve the level of specificity and directness that yours will be able to. For example, one student was able to better articulate her inspiration to join a specific college in her essay by relating a discussion she had with a tour guide who shared her experience during a college visit two years before applying.

You want to be on the lookout for certain aspects that make a school stand out. What do you notice about student engagement on campus? What sticks out to you about qualitative factors like walkability or the overall atmosphere of campus? By doing some preliminary research before arriving on campus, you'll be able to use your time before or after the pre-planned tour or other obligatory activities to seek out the spaces on campus that will reveal much more beneath the surface.

☞ *TIP 42: Don't be shy about connecting with students*

Once you've seen the school and confirmed firsthand that you can thrive there, you should make strong efforts to connect with the school. The best place to start is to reach out to any friends or family who have attended the school, and ask them questions about what their experience was like in the school. These kinds of discussions can help serve as the basis for further research, and provide key insights that can help you stand out when it comes time to actually write about your interest in the school in the application process.

You can also reach out to alumni in your neighborhood, and even to the school's admissions office to learn more about the school's unique offerings. The most valuable resource of all, though, is students attending the school. During your initial visit, you can connect with a student, even through an informal chat, and maintain contact with that student. This way, you can have a "insider" view of what life at the school is like, which is important considering you will potentially be living there for four years.

☞ *TIP 43: Explore alternative options if you can't make a visit*

Obviously, you may not be able to visit every college on your list, even your top school. However, there are still ways that you can demonstrate an elevated level of interest without stepping foot on campus. For instance, schools organize information sessions across the country, whether directly at your local high school via a college fair or similar event, or in local venues such as a YMCA. You can check online to keep updated on whether your top school might be coming to a location near you.

You can even take more active steps such as reaching out directly to faculty in your area of interest to establish lines of communication with people who can not only help provide an extra influential voice in your favor, but also potentially provide research and collaboration opportunities later on down the line.

☞ *TIP 44: Pursue a pre-college/summer program*

After you've performed research and reached out to people who can help direct you to more information about the school, you may want to consider enrolling in summer courses or a dedicated pre-college program offered by the school. Not only do these opportunities allow you to familiarize yourself even more with the campus, but it also enables you to start forming relationships with faculty at the school, who can later potentially provide a letter of reference on your behalf.

Most colleges have many choices of programs ranging from 2 to 7 weeks that can be found on their website. There are summer courses, leadership programs, networking events, sports camps and other boot camps that students can choose from. Many of the longer Pre-college summer programs get filled up as soon as they are opened for enrollment. These longer programs lets you take college level courses for college credits within a short time duration, giving the student an experience of the intensity of college life and academic rigor. In some of the selective colleges, there's an additional selection process to enroll in these programs.

Here again, adequate research and planning is important so that you can pick the right program at the right college, which can align with your interests and passion that will benefit you. Just because a college is considered extremely selective for undergraduate admission doesn't necessarily mean it will offer the most prestigious or rigorous pre-college experience. For example, while the University of Iowa is not generally classified as "extremely competitive" given its 81% acceptance rate, its Iowa Young Writers' Studio summer program is a highly prestigious program that is considered one of the best pre-college programs for budding authors. Similarly, Middlebury College's Summer Language Immersion for Teens programs are top-tier foreign language pre-college opportunities that studies interested in the field should pursue. By choosing the right program and college and successfully completing the program, you will be able to demonstrate to the college that you were very serious about the college and passionate about the area of interest.

Pre-college programs are offered in almost every area: STEM, leadership, arts, architecture, business, medicine, writing, college experience, and foreign languages, among others. Some colleges have specialized programs in emerging areas like robotics, artificial intelligence, neuroscience, and nanotechnology, in addition to the regular college courses in different subjects. It's important to spend time doing adequate research on these programs, taking into account one's area of interest, college reputation, reviews from past students, costs, duration and overall fit, before finalizing a program.

STEP FIVE RECAP:

Demonstrating college interest is a crucial element in helping convince admissions that you are serious about a school.

Campus visits and pre-college programs are not only informative avenues to learning more about a school, but also provide tangible evidence of college interest that will give you an advantage.

Your academic interests should help inform which opportunities you explore, so research programs that will enable you to showcase your passion most effectively.

STEP SIX

Take Your Admissions Interviews Seriously

MYTH: "College interviews are a 'nice to have' that won't have any bearing on my application."

Interviews are not a common part of a student's life. Maybe it could be part of a peer leadership application or the final step in securing a summer job, but for the most part, students are not accustomed to the ins and outs of a successful interview. Unsurprisingly, we have encountered many families who were not even aware that college interviews are a part of the admissions process, let alone how to best prepare for it. With this air of mystery around the interview process, what can families do to get a head start? Well, it starts with knowing what the interview is meant to do.

☞ *TIP 45: Understand that interviews are a two-way street*

A college interview is a chance to show that you're more than just test scores and grades. But at the same time, it's an exchange of information—you learn about the college and the college learns about you. It can last anywhere from 30 to 60 minutes. The interview is just one of many factors in the admissions decision, and admissions directors usually say that the interview is rarely the deciding one. Still, if a borderline student turns out to be impressive, the interviewer has the authority to write a letter in support of the student.

While these interviews are optional, you really should not treat them that way. Because they are much likelier to help you than hurt you, you should never refuse an interview if offered one by a school. Demonstrating interest might therefore mean sacrificing a Saturday afternoon to meet with an alumnus at your fifth or sixth choice school, but it's better to be safe than sorry.

☞ *TIP 46: Make a strong impression*

Plan your outfit before the interview, and dress professionally. Think business or business casual. What you wear will only do so much, though. During the interview, you should be mindful of certain best practices. For example, you should look the interviewer in the eye, use the interviewer's name, shake hands firmly, and project energy and interest.

You should not be late, memorize speeches and render your speech stilted and unnatural, ask questions covered by the college catalog, chew gum, swear or use too much slang, be arrogant (there's a fine line between being confident and boasting!), lie, respond with only yes or no answers, tell the school it's your safety, or bring a parent into the interview.

That's a lot to remember, but for the most part, it all thankfully falls under the category of "common sense."

☞ *TIP 47: Know what questions to expect*

The questions asked by interviewers generally comprise three main categories. The first is what can be called "Tell Me About Yourself." These include extracurricular interests such as sports, and clubs, but also extend to hobbies like reading, scrapbooking, and hiking, or jobs like babysitting. You can also discuss things like your interest in music, or any summer trips you've taken. The key is to talk about the activities that you really enjoy doing, and projecting your enthusiasm in a believably way.

The second category you will encounter is your academic preferences. You might be asked, "What is your favorite subject?" to which you might respond, "I love English!" But then, you have to elaborate on why. You might add, "I love reading and writing; I feel like it pushes me to be a better student." Similarly, you might be asked, "What is your least favorite subject?" to which you might reply, "Chemistry, because math-related subjects have always come hard to me, and I don't easily understand these types of concepts. You want to be honest, but also be professional in explaining your preferences.

You will also hear questions related to your strengths and weaknesses. Some strengths you highlight might be perseverance, integrity, ambition, or a good work ethic. You will also want to be able to readily discuss your weaknesses, though. And be honest! Don't say things like "I'm a perfectionist." Instead, talk about things that can actually be improved. For instance, maybe you get stressed out easily, or your time management skills could use some improvement.

☞ *TIP 48: Show that you care about the school*

You'll also be asked about the school itself, of course. The answer to "Why do you want to attend this school?" will be different for each student, but some common ground would be academics, diversity, resources, and location. You should be equally comfortable answering, "What can you contribute to this school?" Brainstorm how you can get involved and help make the campus community a better place.

Finally, you will be asked if you have any questions. And, absolutely, you should! Come prepared with two or three questions about different topics like special academic programs or study abroad. This will help show your interest.

☞ *TIP 49: Be prepared for anything!*

You should make sure to be ready for random questions as well. "What's your favorite book?" or "Choose three words to best describe yourself" or "Who is your greatest role model?" are all fair game. Regardless of how quirky or intrusive the questions may get, remember to always just be yourself!

Don't try to say things that aren't really true just to impress the admissions officers, and always be honest with yourself and who you are. In the end, the interview is more of a conversation than an interrogation!

☞ *TIP 50: Follow up after the interview*

After the interview, your interviewer will send a brief report to the college that covers what topics you discussed, along with some notes on what observations or questions you may have put forth during the interview. Because it's more of a summary than an evaluation, you don't have to worry about being rated or judged on any specific criteria. Just be your best self, and project the image that you've already established through your application.

As for what you should do after the interview, it's always advisable to send a brief thank-you e-mail to your interviewer. You don't have to be overly elaborate in your follow-up letter, but you should take note of the highlights of your conversation, and communicate in what ways the interview helped clarify any questions you may have had or bolstered your enthusiasm for the school.

☞ *TIP 51: Understand how schools use the interview*

Most schools place some weight on interviews, though some treat them more as informational opportunities for students than as an evaluative measure. Here is a sampling of various top 50 schools' interview policies and purpose.

College	Interview Policy	Interview Purpose
Brown	Required	Evaluative
Columbia	Required	Evaluative
Cornell	Required for Architecture program and the School of Hotel Administration, recommended for the Art program	Informational
Dartmouth	Recommended	Evaluative
Harvard	Required	Evaluative
Princeton	Recommended	Evaluative
University of Pennsylvania	Required	Evaluative
Yale	Recommended	Evaluative
Carnegie Mellon	Recommended	Evaluative
Duke	Recommended	Evaluative
Emory	Recommended	Evaluative
Georgetown University	Required	Evaluative
Johns Hopkins	Optional	Informational
MIT	Strongly recommended	Evaluative

STEP SIX RECAP:

College interviews are a valuable opportunity to learn more about a school, but also to demonstrate your personality and impress admissions.

Before the interview, you should be prepared to answer a range of questions about your academics, extracurriculars, and personality, but you should also come ready with your own set of questions to ask of your interviewer.

The importance of the interview may be weighed differently by different schools, so research the particular approach each school to which you have applied takes to evaluating your interview.

STEP SEVEN

Demonstrate 21ˢᵗ Century Leadership

MYTH: "I have to be Student Council President or the president of a club to show leadership."

"Leadership" is almost a buzzword when it comes to college admissions. At times, it can seem to mean both everything and nothing at all. So what do colleges consider when evaluating a student's leadership?

☞ *TIP 52: Showcase your cultural insights*

First, colleges highly value students who can tap into their unique cultural backgrounds. In addition to drawing upon the values of their own cultures, however, it is also important to demonstrate a willingness to seek to understand and learn from the cultures of others. In order to accomplish these goals, students should pursue opportunities to showcase cultural competence, both within their own cultures and among those of their peers. And when it comes time to apply, they should shine a spotlight on their international background and experiences.

This means that students should take special note of opportunities for these types of culturally rich experiences. Traveling abroad on a foreign service trip or even maintaining contact with an international pen pal can open a door to gaining the globally minded lens that colleges appreciate.

☞ *TIP 53: Become a healthy skeptic*

Colleges also prize the ability to assess a high volume of information. Students should regularly question the world around them to seek deeper understandings and thoughtfully evaluate materials and perspectives, rather than accepting things at face value. This can be demonstrated by taking on challenges through extracurricular activities or research that help stretch a student's ability to critically assess their surroundings and their own place within it.

By applying a more critical lens to the world around you, you will be able to discover new understandings and insights that you might not have even considered before. A traditional classroom environment might sometimes cultivate a dullness that makes you readily accept everything you are taught without questioning it, but independent reading and research can reveal an entire spectrum of alternative points of view that can illuminate your own perspectives.

☞ *TIP 54: Be able to hold a conversation with everyone and anyone*

Colleges are also looking for evidence of cross-cultural communication skills. Students should effectively exchange ideas with peers and adults from different backgrounds — either virtually or in person — and have the skills to enter new communities and spaces.

When you enter college, you will join a new space full of people whose backgrounds and beliefs may differ dramatically from your own, and so it is crucial to build the interpersonal skills early on that will enable you to foster healthy, respectful relationships with people of all stripes and creeds.

We have encountered students who told us that college was their first time interacting with a student with a different religion, sexual orientation, or native language. While this "culture shock" can be harmless, it can also be reflective of a lack of substantial, meaningful attempts to have discovered and embraced those differences earlier in life. Because culture shock can sometimes manifest in unwelcome ways that harm the experience of everyone involved, colleges want to admit students they feel comfortable will not just be tolerant of difference, but actively seek it out. They want to know that students are able to adopt alternate perspectives. Students should demonstrate curiosity and empathy, and be able to show compassion for the perspectives of others, through volunteering abroad or lending a helping hand in their own communities. You can show that to colleges so that they won't question it.

☞ *TIP 55: Be bold*

In demonstrating your leadership, you should not be afraid to take risks. No one ever inspired a community or changed the world by following the crowd, so you should always think outside the box in any endeavor you take on. This means that if you're president of yearbook, for instance, you don't have to do the same things that your predecessor did.

You can put your personal spin on tasks that are normally considered prosaic, and in doing so, discover your unique contribution as a leader that will last long beyond your tenure.

☞ *TIP 56: Know your limits*

While boldly taking on new ventures shows your character in a way that colleges value, they also want students to be able to acknowledge their own limitations. Students should understand that their knowledge is not infinite and appreciate how much more there is to learn about the world.

Students should understand the massive scope of the world and its complexities, and seek help when a particularly challenging roadblock emerges. Students don't have to pretend to know it all!

☞ *TIP 57: Be original*

"Think different" is more than just a famous advertising slogan, it's a lifestyle. Students should endeavor to find alternative, unique solutions to existing problems and be able to envision the world differently from how it currently exists.

In your in-class work and outside of school, your efforts should reflect your willingness to think big, not just to think in the "now."

☞ *TIP 58: Use technology for good*

Students should exhibit technological literacy. Students should utilize and explore existing technologies to communicate and collaborate with others, and to learn and share new ideas and information. Not all students will create new technologies, but all students can discover new uses for technologies that help them and others navigate their worlds. While many students are already technologically aware through such mediums as social networks, there's a marked difference between using technology to casually check in on what everyone else is doing and using technology to change the conversation in meaningful ways.

Broadly speaking, then, leadership can be viewed as students' individual and collective actions to change the world for the better. In our world of increased interdependence, enormous complexity, and accelerating change, an understanding and practice of leadership is essential.

STEP SEVEN RECAP:

Colleges want to see that you have demonstrated leadership in your school and local community.

Leadership can be expressed in multiple ways, including through concerted collaboration and innovative problem solving.

STEP EIGHT

Make Your Recommendation Letters Count

MYTH: "I should seek out teachers who gave me my best grades to write my recommendation letter."

This step will require come careful planning. Recommendation letters are secretly one of the most important items that admission committees evaluate, because they provide a rare glimpse into a student's overall fit from an outsider's point of view. We have seen many students get admitted into top schools with just above average academic credentials but really strong recommendation letters that made a big difference to their application.

We have also seen students with very strong academic credentials who have not been admitted to their desired schools because they did go above and beyond with their recommendation letters. This usually happens when students do not plan enough and put the effort needed, because they get confident and complacent about their chances due to their strong grades and good standardized test scores. However, recommendation letters can tip the scales in profound ways.

☞ *TIP 59: Know the right number of letters for you*

One question that always comes up is how many recommendation letters are too many. A general rule of thumb is that above four is too many unless the school has specifically requested additional ones, which rarely happens. Some schools (also very few) state very clearly that the students should not submit more than two.

If there's a clear instruction from the school, you should abide by it. Outside of these schools, you should consider sending three to four recommendation letters along with your application.

☞ *TIP 60: Make your letters match your area of interest...*

First, pick the teacher and the subject that is most relevant to your college major that you are applying to. Obviously, if you are applying for science or engineering, do not choose the recommendation letter from history or social studies just because your grade was higher in that subject.

☞ *TIP 61: ...but make sure you show diversity as well*

However, because colleges want to see diversity in your academic strengths, don't stack the deck with teachers who all taught a similar set of subjects. For instance, a STEM candidate would be well-served by choosing an English or foreign language teacher for a second letter of recommendation.

You'll need to plan ahead – this also means you need to make sure you choose the subjects and teachers ahead of time and put in the hard work and effort to do well in that subject. You should also make sure to engage and connect with your teachers. Ask questions in class, spend time with the teacher outside class hours getting help on homework, and perhaps even ask the teacher to challenge you with harder work or questions to show that you really are interested in that particular subject.

☞ *TIP 62: Help your counselor out*

Another important factor is the recommendation letter from the school counselor. Most public schools in the US have hundreds of students in every grade and only a few counselors. Hence, you usually get very limited facetime with counselors at school. Regardless, the counselors do send a recommendation letter for every student. Hence, it's entirely up to you to make sure that these counselors know who you are and the aspects that differentiate your profile and activities that you have done at school and outside school.

☞ *TIP 63: Make a brag sheet*

As you near the end of junior year, most schools ask for a self-profile and parents' input, which you may have to answer through a list of questions. Guidance counselors use this input to write their recommendation letter, so it's important to take the time and effort to think through and answer the questions comprehensively so that you are able to articulate all the things that might help differentiate you from your peers. We have seen many students put something together in the last day of submission and treat it more like a homework assignment, but it really should take quite a bit of thought.

Therefore, you should consider a range of questions: Have you engaged with the counselor regularly to get advice and suggestions on college choices? Does the counselor know you and what you have done in and outside school? Have you taken the time and effort to fill up the profile questionnaire from the school? Have you discussed with your parents to make sure that they have provided the right input? The answer to all of these should be "Yes!"

☞ *TIP 64: Seek supplemental letters of recommendation*

You will also want to consider obtaining a recommendation letter from someone outside school. This could be from someone who knows you well and what you are capable of, and can truly add a perspective or dimension outside of your academic strengths. Possible choices to consider are someone from the venue in which you did completed a summer activity or internship related to your passion, a group or organization where you made a difference to through leadership, volunteering, charitable activity or community service, an athletic coach, adviser, or supervisor, someone who may be connected to the college in some capacity and knows you well, or a professor from a pre-college program or course.

This last one is usually a difficult one to obtain because college professors are extremely busy and usually do not write recommendation letters, or there may be college policies that restrict them from doing so. However, if you are able to get a letter from a college professor who has seen you attend his or her course and perform well in that class, it's a great way to demonstrate to a college that you are able to adapt well in the college environment, you are able to challenge yourself, and you have proven that you can perform in college-level courses. This is seen as a distinguishing trait to the admission committee.

STEP EIGHT RECAP:

Your recommendation letters provide an alternative perspective of your qualifications, so choose which teachers will be your recommenders wisely.

Your guidance counselor will write you a letter of recommendation as well, so it is important to establish a positive relationship with him or her.

You can include supplemental recommendation letters from people outside of school, including athletic coaches and supervisors from your volunteering or employment, and these individuals can help flesh out your profile.

STEP NINE

Make Your Application Impactful

MYTH: "There are too many applicants, so admissions counselors don't really read all the essays."

There are two reasons why colleges ask you to write an essay as part of your application: to show the admissions committee who you are (in addition to what you've done), and to show the admissions committee you can write. But there's a lot more that goes into this than you might expect.

☞ *TIP 65: Tell a compelling story*

"It was a dark and stormy night..."
   You would probably toss aside any thriller or mystery novel that began this way. It's a painful cliché that tells you nothing about the person who wrote it, and reveals nothing unique about their worldview. We use fiction as an escape from the humdrum, and so the last thing we want to encounter is a work that only magnifies our boredom. Students would be wise to take this advice into account for their own application essays.
   It's easier said than done, however. For most students, the main essay that you will submit to most or all of your choice schools (known as the personal statement or personal essay) poses some immediate challenges. First and foremost is that it's simply uncharted territory. Students are accustomed to writing about other topics in subjects far removed from their own day-to-day experiences: think Iago's betrayal in "Othello," the finer distinctions between adenosine triphosphate and adenosine diphosphate, or the causes of the War of 1812. When students are suddenly asked to write

about themselves, even the most astute and eloquent writers among them might wonder what on earth to write about, and how to write about it.

The best place to start is with your own preferences. Think about media, whether fiction or nonfiction, that grabbed you from the very beginning and dared you to look away. Ask yourself what specific traits those works all had in common. Was it a gripping plot? Was it high stakes? Was it interesting wordplay? Whatever it was, it was compelling. And that is what your essay needs to be from the get-go in order to earn and maintain the interest of the person reading it. You don't know who that person will be, but chances are high that they'll be just as critical of you as you were of the last novel you read that began with the line, "Once upon a time…"

☞ *TIP 66: Draw upon unique experiences as you brainstorm*

Over time, your amazing, once-in-a-lifetime experiences of past years start to dull, your recollection of them becoming hazy and eventually, perhaps even nonexistent. But what to you is just a dusty shoebox of memories might, to a college, be a fascinating treasure trove.

So be an open book about the special things you have done, even if they were not necessarily recent. This might involve global or international experience, for example. Have you lived or studied outside the United States? How has that experience shaped you or helped you determine what you want to pursue in college? Don't assume that just because those experiences might not have taken place during high school that they are not worth sharing.

Even after reading the example essays provided later in this section, you might still be wondering exactly how to capture your essential self in written form. But sometimes the best topic for the personal statement or best framing for a supplement essay just comes down to recognizing the "obvious" traits you possess that you might not have considered worthy of inclusion, let alone being made the topic of an essay. In other words, sometimes "obvious" is the best place to start!

Regardless, it all begins with brainstorming. Start by listing as many things you can think or that are creative and interesting about you, using the aforementioned ideas as a jumping-off point. You can even ask a friend for some tips if you have difficulty evaluating yourself. Then, list some things you possess, objects in your home that are of special meaning to you, and that let your personality shine. You'd be surprised by how interesting the stories behind those items might be! Finally, list any hobbies, passions, quotes, fictional or non-fictional characters who inspire you, or anything else that you think represents who you are and what you value.

☞ *TIP 67: Celebrate your diversity*

This particular tip is an inherent part of any effective brainstorming session, but is of enough importance to merit a special discussion. Colleges are interested in getting to know you in all the ways that you might already imagine, such as grades and extracurriculars. However, they are also invested in ensuring that their campuses are diverse, heterogeneous environments. For example, do you belong to a minority group? What has been your experience in growing up? How does your experience as a minority help contribute to the diversity of a college campus?

Also know that diversity can come in many forms, from ethnic background to religious faith to political orientation, so even if your diversity can't be captured in the check of a box, find ways to showcase what makes you special. It might be a quirky hobby or a unique physical attribute, but no matter what it is, don't shy away from shining a spotlight on it.

☞ *TIP 68: Focus not just on "what" but "how"*

College admission counselors are eager to read about your ideas, but they also want to know about your overall sense of style. Thus, what you write about and how you write about it are necessarily intertwined. The notable film critic Roger Ebert once said about cinema, "It's not what a movie is about, it's how it is about it." While we might more strongly endorse the idea that the "what" is of paramount importance for a strong application essay, we also recognize the wisdom of Ebert's words. After all, you've probably watched an untold number of action-packed movies full of dazzling explosions and boundless intrigue that somehow still left you falling asleep by the end. At the same time, you probably also distinctly remember movies that were more quiet and more intimate, yet managed to keep you on the edge of your seat.

This difference is where the "how" comes in. The same way that a film director can imprint their own unique stamp on a movie that distinguishes it from the competition, you can use your essay as a vehicle to showcase your own trademark as a writer. For some, this might mean the use of abundant literary flourish that showcases their poetic side. For others, this might involve creative wordplay that reflects the writer's sarcastic wit. Regardless, your essay should reveal your unique style in a way that goes beyond what the topic is, and into how you decide to present it.

☞ *TIP 69: Organize your thoughts*

Once you have a sense of what your topic and how you will

present it, the next step is to think about structure. Here, you can take some decidedly untraditional approaches. For instance, you might think of starting your narrative in a place that is not the very beginning of the actual story, also known as beginning "in medias res" or "in the middle of things." You could then circle back to the events that led to the place your essay opened with.

One particularly effective approach is to "bookend" your narrative, ending your story with a thought that refers back to an image or idea from the introduction. It's not generally a good idea to let your essay end on an unresolved note, so this approach could make achieving that satisfying sense of conclusion a bit easier. Another approach is to answer the "So what?" question. That is, addressing the broader implications or significance of your narrative to illustrate how your story had far-reaching impacts beyond what might seem immediately apparent.

☞ *TIP 70: Show colleges the real you, but don't overshare*

Some colleges allow you to submit a 1-2 minute video recording along with the application. Online portals like ZeeMee have partnered with over 200 schools and provide tools for students to film, edit, and submit a video message as a supplement to the various essays they have already written. This can make a big difference when the college can associate a face with a name, instead of just relying on a paper application, and provides yet another vehicle for you to showcase something unique about yourself.

While we encourage being an open book in your applications, though, there are limits to what you should reasonably share with a committee of people who are, in the end, complete strangers. Successful topics can be very revealing, but you should only reveal as much as you need to get your point across. Don't dwell too much on the ugly details of a trying experience, for example, at the expense of showing how you grew from it and emerged stronger for it. This applies to any video submissions as well, which should ideally present you in a professional light that enhances, rather than detracts from, the overall presentation you want colleges to see.

☞ *TIP 71: Invite others on your journey*

Finally, let at least three other people, like a parent, an English teacher, and a trusted friend, read your essay. You don't need to implement all the advice you receive, but a fresh perspective from someone who knows you well can provide needed insight.

☞ *TIP 72: Be open to different "styles" of essays*

The following is a sample of student personal statement that we have worked on with students. As you will find, there is no formula for a "perfect" essay, but rather a range of possibilities for how you can express yourself and how you can contribute to a college's campus. These examples will reflect this diversity, and should serve as examples to help inspire and motivate you as you go about drafting your own essays, but you should not model your own essays entirely after the examples that follow.

☞ *TIP 73: Be specific in the details you include*

PERSONAL STATEMENT EXAMPLE 1

"My face strains, with furrowed brows and pursed lips, frozen in place for the past ten minutes. Suddenly, I hear the director yell "Cut!" and am relieved to finally feel the sweet sensation of movement again. The sacrifices we make for art. The art in this case was a student-made film for the annual High School Film Challenge, a statewide competition that tasks amateur filmmakers with scripting, storyboarding, filming, and editing a short concept film based on an assigned theme...all within ten days. What impulse led me to this masochistic endeavor? Simply put – love.

My love of acting was born the moment I stepped foot on a movie set. During my summers in India, my uncle [NAME OMITTED], who has directed and starred in over forty Indian films, would show me around the studio. For a five-year-old, the chance to see behind the curtain of sets, props, costumes, and cameras (and lots of Bollywood choreography!) was an awesome rush. I was immediately captivated by the actors, who were responsible for making what appeared to be flat, crude representations of real-life landscapes come alive. Ultimately, actors allow the storytellers and directors to convey their creative messages to the audience, and from a young age, I wanted to be exactly that kind of vessel: I wanted to be a famous actor.

I threw myself into acting, taking part in my elementary school's stage productions and even writing my own screenplays. It wasn't until high school, though, that I truly sought to challenge myself. I joined my school's Speech and Debate Team, participating in Dramatic Interpretation and Improvisational Acting. My first role, that of the charming but psychopathic Patrick Bateman in the film adaptation of "American Psycho," was an interesting experience, to say the least. Playing a character so far removed from my own personality forced me to learn how to better empathize with others, regardless of their unsavory backgrounds. I've always believed that actors are the most emotionally generous people on earth because they inhabit another person's point of view every day, but this role really put me to the test. In the end, though, it was worth it, and I won my first award in Dramatic Interpretation.

Emboldened by my success in Speech and Debate, I set my sights even higher, working toward acting outside of school in my own original productions. A friend of mine was in the process of writing a script for the Film Challenge, and (with a great deal of trepidation) I approached him to ask if he needed an actor. It turned out I was exactly who he was looking for, and became the lead. After reading his newest draft, I felt a knot form in the pit of my stomach: the entire film was a one-take close-up of my face with my audio monologue in the background. In the past, I played larger-than-life characters like Patrick Bateman and my self-styled superhero "Testosterone Man," and now I'd be playing someone who had to tell the entire story with only his face. I practiced for hours in front of a mirror, brooding and glaring and grimacing to perfection until my face went numb. By the time the cameras started rolling, I'd completely studied my character, and all the nerves dissipated.

Approximately thirty takes later, my work was done, and we sent our little film out into the universe, expecting very little in return. Two months passed, and to my surprise, the universe conspired to place our film in the Top 25 among the hundreds of submissions throughout the state. To be recognized for my hard work was just the cherry on top of actually putting in the hard work and growing immeasurably as an actor. In movies, actors pretend to be in with their co-stars, and they often fool the audience. The trick, you see, is not loving the actor, but loving the acting."

This is an excellent personal statement because it shows this candidate has had a tangible impact on those around them.

The statement keeps the reader engaged by giving a meaningful story with background, context, conflict, and resolution. It also provides a peek into a unique kind of artistic experience.

This is a good model for someone who is interested in showcasing their characteristics in an engaging way. The essay is focused on broad ideas, with a concrete progression of accomplishments to back up the writer's plans. This person is a doer, not a dreamer.

The writer shows a depth of knowledge and strong analytical reasoning skills that go far beyond the norm, especially in their description of finding solutions to difficult, trying circumstances. This type of statement would make admissions committees want to admit this student because they has demonstrated unique drive and vision for their craft.

This statement, therefore, will inspire members of the admissions committee to act on the applicant's behalf because they has successfully reached beyond expectations.

☞ *TIP 74: Be creative in your approach, but make sure it fits you*

PERSONAL STATEMENT EXAMPLE 2

"So...what are you?" Every time I'm faced with this question, I pause, already knowing your reaction before I've uttered a single word. "I'm Russian and Haitian – basically, I'm half black and half white." As I respond, studying your widening eyes, I already anticipate your reply. "Wow, that's interesting!" I, once the fascinating enigma, now the circus curiosity. Unsurprisingly, this remark never fails to suddenly put an awkward pall over the entire conversation. And I can always count on this reaction; the few exceptions are actually the ones that unnerve me. I've learned to live with this occasional bout of condescension, however, because I've always taken pride in my unique background. Even as far back as my infancy, I'd happily chant beside my parents, "Dada is brown, mama is white, and I am peach!"

Our conversation continues. To further pique your interest, I'll sometimes add, "And I'm also both Christian and Jewish." Again, the requisite, "Wow, that's interesting!" Again, the unmistakable cloud of awkwardness befalls us. Easter must be a weird time for him, I hear you thinking. His parents must not go to the same church. You couldn't be farther from the truth. As a child, I attended Sunday school and sometimes even regular church services with both of my parents in an all-black Christian church. Then, as I entered my adolescent years, I went to Hebrew school three days a week. I learned the Torah and sang in a language I did not even know. At thirteen, I even celebrated my bar mitzvah and was given a Torah of my own.

I've come to know myself and to know God because of this mix of religion and culture, not in spite of it. For instance, my dual religious identity has granted me a strong, balanced sense of morality. My Christian faith has taught me the importance of sacrifice through its teachings on being generous with my time and my money, imparting the notion of doing unto others what I would have them do unto me (not always an easy code to live by!). Similarly, my Jewish faith has taught me a different side of sacrifice through its emphasis on dietary restrictions and a disciplined abstinence from work that all must abide by. It's perhaps a bit of an oversimplification, but by combining what Christianity tells us to do with what Judaism tells us not to do, I've been able to develop a more ethical mindset in everything that I do. In trying times, I can draw upon my diverse background to make the right decision.

And it's because of this upbringing that I've become

confident in who I am. Both the Star of David and the crucifix are firmly affixed to my necklace and rest on my tan chest. When people ask me what I am, I give a simple answer, a simple label. Inside, though, I know that I'm more than just a set of demographic checkboxes; I represent progress. It was only fifty years ago that Loving v. Virginia decriminalized interracial marriage in the United States, and it remained illegal in Africa until the end of apartheid in 1994. In time, the labels that categorize and separate us will fade, along with the judgment and pretension that often accompany them. My mixed heritage has given me a special vantage point: one that focuses less on how we are different and more on that greater part that we share – and it seems the world has its eyes fixed in that direction too.

Our conversation draws to a close. Having satisfied your curiosity, I become the questioner. It's your turn now.

"So...what are you?"

This personal statement is constructed like a poem: there is a rhythm to it that draws the reader in; there is also wordplay and the construction of a somewhat mysterious self-portrait.

This applicant had an impressive GPA and test scores, so he could be a risk-taker with the personal statement. This essay stands out because it is more artfully designed than other statements. This is a good strategy if you are sure of your standardized scores or if you are applying to a reach school and so are trying to get yourself noticed.

An experimental personal statement such as this is just as likely to succeed as to fail, because some admissions committee members value creativity while others will be put off by the lack of specific details. In its uniqueness, it is unclear how difficult this statement was to write; most admissions committee members will probably give the candidate the benefit of the doubt and see it as highly original rather than a series of clichés. However, this approach is not for everyone.

☞ *TIP 75: Take a risk, and commit to it*

PERSONAL STATEMENT EXAMPLE 3

"It's a good thing you came here at this time. If you waited a bit longer you might have died." As relieving as it was to hear that I skirted death, those words also forced me to imagine how things could've turned out had we hit a red light or gotten stuck in traffic. My parents' hysterics over almost losing their nine-year-old little boy hinted that they'd felt the same. Within moments, I was being prepped for surgery.

Sensing my unease, the surgeon tried to lighten the mood with some jokes. Unfortunately, they were all about how much he hated his job — not the most comforting thing to hear when someone's about to cut into you. Interrupting his stand-up routine, I asked exactly why I required surgery.

"One of your organs got inflamed, then started to swell and block other organs from doing their job."

Unsatisfied, I prodded further. "What organ is it?"

After a solemn pause, he leaned in and whispered into my ears: "Your balls."

I started cracking up. A flood of thoughts rushed into my head. What would my epitaph be?

"[NAME OMITTED], betrayed and murdered by his testes."

How would people react at my funeral? I pictured my loved ones attempting to suppress their giggles as the priest delivered the eulogy of how my scrotum got the best of me.

Unfortunately, I was still stuck in the hospital for the night, which gave me plenty of time to think. To think about how all the terror I'd just felt dissipated owing to a joke about my penis.

I experienced firsthand how comedy could change the tone: light to dark, uncomfortable to inviting, serious to easygoing. I thought about how a lot of comics say some of the most terrible and shocking things, but nobody gets mad. Instead, they listen, and they laugh. Then once the laughter has subsided, they reflect. And with that, I discovered my passion. I wanted to become a comic ... or at least funny.

As much as comedy relies on an audience, it's even more useful in day-to-day life. Armed with only a joke, you can shape the tone of a conversation and control the flow. There the laughs come easily because you're not expected to be funny.

On stage it isn't the same because you're expected to make people laugh. You're expected to be charming, or at least confident, but that doesn't mean you can't be raw. There's a reason why Jon Stewart and John Oliver, both comedians, are respected as news sources. Good comics will make fun of everything. They don't need to lie because making someone laugh while breaking bad news is the ultimate sugarcoat.

The great thing about comedy is that, like anything else, it gets better with practice and ultimately, so did I. I learned to use this in many uncomfortable and high-pressure situations to ease tension and control the flow in a positive direction.

If someone is sad it would cheer them up. If one of my classes got boring it would reinvigorate interest. If I was ever nervous or had to give a presentation, a joke not only makes me less tense but puts the audience out of an awkward situation.

For years, I was an introvert. I felt more comfortable in the dim light of my computer monitor than in the company of people. But now, there is no reason for me to be afraid because if you can laugh at yourself, nothing really bothers you anymore. Plus when you get a laugh out of someone, it's like an adrenaline rush that melts away all fear, all anxiety.

And so, in an ironic sense, it was the incident with my testicles that helped me grow a pair."

This personal statement is mostly humorous in tone, but offers a deep insight into the candidate's unique ability to overcome obstacles. While the subject matter is somewhat shocking and even potentially offensive, it overcomes those considerations with a light touch toward the heavy subject matter and with a consistent voice.

This particular approach is, like the prior example, a risky one, but it can pay off if you are serious about committing to the tone you have established, whether humorous or otherwise.

While the personal statement is the biggest beast to slay, a horde of minions lies close behind. The writing, in other words, is not done. In fact, it's just begun. We are talking, of course, about the dreaded supplement essays, college-specific prompts that individual schools have designed, unlike the personal statement (for which student can choose their own prompt). Not every college has one, and some even have multiple, but because these essays are geared toward particular schools, it is essential to have a clear strategy and personalized approach for each one. It's also important to stay on top of the various prompts, because there are enough of them that you might get lost if you're not careful.

☞ *TIP 76: Make a system to triage your supplement essays*

As you go about planning the various essays, you can add them to your college application spreadsheet, and designate each a specific color based on what type of prompt it is.

School	Common App?	Sent ACT	Sent SAT	Deadline	Word Limit	Prompt	Done (Y/N)	Notes
Boston University	Y	X	X		250	What about being a student at Boston University mos		
Carnegie Mellon University	Y	X	X		1 page	Please submit a one page, single-spaced essay that		
Duke University	Y	X	X		250	Duke University seeks a talented, engaged student b		
					150	If you are applying to the Trinity College of Arts & Sci		
Georgia Institute of Technology	Y	X	X		150	Beyond rankings, location, and athletics, why are you		
Johns Hopkins University	Y	X	X		400	Successful students at Johns Hopkins make the bigg		
Northeastern University	Y	X	X		None			
Northwestern University	Y	X	X		300	Other parts of your application give us a sense for ho		
New York University	Y	X	X		400	We would like to know more about your interest in NY		
Princeton University	Y	X	X		150	Please briefly elaborate on one of your extracurricula		
					150	Please tell us how you have spent the last two summ		
					150	Your favorite book and its author; Your favorite book a		
Rice University	Y	X	X		150	Please briefly elaborate on one of your extracurricula		
					150	With the understanding that the choice of academic s		
					250	How did you first learn about Rice University, and wh		
					500	The quality of Rice's academic life and the Residentia		
University of Michigan	Y	X	X		300	Everyone belongs to many different communities		
					500	Describe the unique qualities that attract you to th		
					150	If you could only do one of the activities you have list		
University of Notre Dame	Y	X	X		175	What excites you about the University of Notre Dame		
University of Pennsylvania	Y	X	X		175	How will you explore your intellectual and academic i		
University of Texas-Austin	N	X	X		500	What was the environment in which you were raised?		
					250	Do you believe your academic record (transcript infor		
					250	How do you show leadership in your life? How do you		
					250	If you could have any career, what would it be? Why?		
University of Virginia	Y	X	X		250	What work of art, music, science, mathematics, or lite		
Villanova University	Y	X	X		250	At Villanova, we believe that it is our similarities that r		

In general, these supplements fall under three main types: the "Why Us" essay that asks you to explain why you are drawn to a particular school and how that school can benefit you, the "Activities" essay that asks you to expand on one particular extracurricular that is of special importance to you, and the "Creative" essay that can literally be about anything the college wants. One essay this past year from Wake Forest University, for example, tasked students with making a "Top Ten" list of anything they wanted. It's an opportunity to have some fun, but brings along its own host of perils if students have too much fun with it. In the spreadsheet, the "Why Us?" essay style is a red color, the "Activities" essay a blue color, and the "Creative" style of supplement essays a green color. You can devise your own system to best suit your needs. Regardless, there will likely be a fair number of essays to juggle, so organization is key!

Here are some examples of supplement essays that fall under traditional categories you might be asked to write on:

☞ *TIP 77: Tie the school's offerings to your own personal aims*

SUPPLEMENT ESSAY 1: The "Why Us?" Essay (University of Pennsylvania)

"I might've been an inexperienced ninth grader, but I was teeming with confidence. I had it all planned out. An empty kitchen floor. A 77 step-by-step guide I compiled from tutorial videos and online forums. A non-static wristband that would prevent me from destroying my more sentimentally than economically valuable equipment. I pulled my socks off, touched the metal doorknob, and took on the challenge of building my first computer.

Did I have to build it on Christmas Day as my parents were getting ready to host our entire family for the afternoon? No. But the anticipation of over six months of planning, part-picking, and pleading compelled me to spread a power supply unit, a hard drive, a processor, a motherboard, a fan, two memory sticks, a graphics card, and a bundle of cables across the kitchen table. The Christmas ham would have to find a new home for the day.

I spent the whole morning on my hands and knees, occasionally getting up to touch the doorknob, beyond terrified of transmitting a static shock to a board or processor and frying everything I'd begged my parents for. What some would consider boring or even torturous – screwing in parts, plugging in wires, sorting cables – was the time of my life. As equipment gradually moved from the table into my magical metal enclosure, I already started to see myself as a bona fide computer engineer. Suddenly, I was thrust into the tech operating room armed only with a Google-search education. I nearly panicked when I realized my confidence turned complacency caused me to bend a handful of the 904 fragile pins on the bottom of the central processor.

Luckily, a Christmas miracle occurred, and no damage was done. Since that fateful day, my messy little hobby has become a true passion. At Penn Engineering, I'll be able to further explore my interests in computer architecture and semiconductor physics — areas in which Penn stands at the forefront. Beyond the school's incredible range of academic offerings, its research opportunities also represent the cutting edge of inquiry into nascent fields like nanoelectronic devices and biotechnology. Despite my years of DIY projects and learning as I go, I still haven't been exposed to the lion's share of what makes computer engineering such an exciting arena. For instance, while I've built many computers and robots, I haven't been able to plumb the depths of the architecture that powers those machines. That will change at Penn.

Through labs and research centers like PRECISE and its investigation into cyber-physical and embedded systems, I'll actually see the inner workings of the technology that surrounds us. Best of all, I'll be able to deepen my engagement with computer engineering under the guidance and expertise of Penn's world-class faculty, whose uniquely inclusive attitude toward undergraduate research makes the school such an appealing institution. Not only will this type of hands-on, collaborative study bolster my working knowledge of new technologies, but it will also enable me to forge my own research into uncharted territory moving forward.

Research is only one piece of the puzzle, though. Ultimately, I want to channel the skills and knowledge I gain at Penn toward real-world solutions to the problems — technological, medical, ethical, and otherwise — that society continues to grapple with. I'm eager to apply the abstract to the concrete, and bolster my working experience in the field.

Faculty-led firms such as Innolign and Znetics, products of Penn's own UPstart Program, are leading the charge in areas like bioengineering, and it's incredibly exciting to see them take shape in what would be my future backyard.

Four years ago, as I toiled and tinkered with my very first computer, I felt like I was making magic. At Penn, I'll learn the true wizardry behind the technology that surrounds us, and maybe one day, craft my very own magic for the world to enjoy."

This essay is successful because it achieves a level of specificity that most students do not reach. Instead of referring to generic, broad offerings that a school promises, it takes care to identify tangible programs that the student is able to tie into their own academic and personal goals.

☞ *TIP 78: Emphasize the impact you have had*

SUPPLEMENT ESSAY 2: The "Activities" Essay (University of Michigan)

"Right as I sat down with a pack of elementary school students I'd never met before, they rattled off their ideas for what they needed in their humble after-school space. New games; the old ones are missing pieces. No, we need a better reading area. What about a spot for art or computers? I was visiting the Valley Settlement House, a local organization that provides child care for families in need, to discuss my Eagle Scout project with the director. To my surprise, she didn't simply hand me a predetermined outline of her vision; instead, she granted me the freedom to formulate any plan I saw fit and released me to the students. After years of planning meetings, leading trips, helping with other projects, and fundraising for my Troop, I never appreciated the effort behind and impact of a large undertaking until I finished my own project.

Armed with a blank slate and an array of inputs from the children who use the recreational area, I had to determine which improvements to prioritize. The real challenge was deciding what could turn a bland, uninviting space into a place where students would want to spend their afternoons, keeping them out of trouble elsewhere. And so I began developing an outline with the ambitious goals of setting up computers, installing decorations and carpets and painting the walls. In order to make this dream a reality, I had to get creative.

My first stop was my school's computer science teacher, who happened to have spare laptops to donate. Next was my town's "WorkMom" email chain, where I sought donations and volunteers. As the project took shape, I marshaled the resources of every person willing to help, whether it was a neighbor, church parishioner, or friend, raising over $1,000 and recruiting the assistance of 20 volunteers. LeBron posters replaced Twilight ones, vibrant maps brought bleak walls to life, and the room in such dire need of a makeover started to come together. By the end of 1,500 hours of service, we amassed more games, art, books, and computers than even my most optimistic projections anticipated.

My immediate goal was to attain Eagle Scout rank, and I'm indeed proud of that accomplishment. But my most lasting and meaningful contribution wasn't to myself. It was to the smiling children, eager to embark on their own creative journeys in art, learning, fun, and life."

This essay shines in its ability to showcase how the student not only endeavored to make a difference in their local community, but how they utilized the various resources around them to make it happen.

Demonstrating your ability to succeed on your own merits can work for this type of essay, but more often than not, a better approach is to demonstrate how you can collaborate with others to achieve shared goals as a community, not as an individual.

☞ *TIP 79: It's okay to be weird*

SUPPLEMENT ESSAY 3: The "Creative" Essay (University of Chicago)

"In the hands of social media lovers, a cell phone's primary function is to display humanity's greatest invention: internet memes. And if you dedicate your social media time to explore the treasure troves of memes like I do, then you must be familiar with the nature of memes, especially when they happen to cross over into everyday life. To illustrate...

Memes protec: Some days, I find myself exhausted. Memes, however, keep me smiling even after a day of failed experiments. On days when I'm troubled with a math problem, a simple Google search of math memes reminds me that I'm not the only one banging my head against a brick wall. Take, for example, the irrational number pi and its non-real cousin "i." On my math homework, I find these two cousins insulting each other: "Be rational!" "Get real!!" On other days, when I fail to advance to the elimination rounds at national debate tournaments, debate memes temper my disappointment with laughs about the quirks and struggles that many debaters encounter.

Memes attac: I have many opinions on a wide range of topics. Politics, science, movies – you name it. Sometimes I can even get a little bit passionate when discussing them. Memes lower my emotional temperature by acting as a shorthand for getting my opinion across, however critical, with a gentler touch. Most debates on figures like Donald Trump end in tears and anguish, all parties stomping off with venom in their hearts. But memes can humanize even the most polarizing of figures. After all, we as a country were united in amusement as our president, against all better wisdom, stared directly into the solar eclipse. No matter how controversial the topic, memes help us laugh by poking fun rather than pointing a loaded gun.

But most importantly... memes connec: In today's technological utopia, it's effortless to communicate with friends via the web. Internet memes have become the preferred mode for friends to share jokes with each other. Whether at the lunchroom table or on Snapchat, my friends and I can always depend on a hilarious dancing hot dog to brighten up our day. On a more serious level, though, memes can help shape entire social movements. Symbols like the Babadook have become, through a combination of happenstance and sheer will, the face of entire classes of people. Were it not for Netflix's meme-worthy typographical oversight, the LGBT community would not be able to rally around this most unlikely of queer icons.

Throughout my exploration of social media, I've realized that as with bottle-flipping and Palpatine's rise to the Senate, memes are temporary. They come and go. They shine brightly and then burn out. But while one meme might quickly give way to the next, its imprint remains. Memes are a rotating chain of arms and mails, and just like any other form of armor, shield us and remind us that we're all more alike than we are unalike."

This essay, which granted the student the ability to write about any topic of their choosing, is successful because it reveals the student's own quirky and fun personality through "meme" references. It might not discuss the topic in a particularly accessible way, but that isn't the point: it reflects the student's ability to thoughtfully explore a common topic like memes and put their unique spin on it.

STEP NINE RECAP:

Your essays are your largest canvas on which to communicate who you are to colleges, so use them as an opportunity to be both expressive and impressive.

Your personal statement and college-specific supplement essays can take many forms in terms of presentation, but they should all work together to reveal your personality, intellectual vitality, and (as applicable) future plans.

Beyond essays, you can further express your unique traits and skills through avenues such as ZeeMee.

STEP TEN

Strategize Your Way In

MYTH: "Better to wait until regular decision in order to show colleges my full first-semester senior year grades and maximize my chances."

When it comes to college admissions, getting in involves more than just a strong application. How you apply can also make a dramatic difference as well.

☞ *TIP 80: Know the different admissions pathways*

Colleges generally have two sets of deadlines by which you submit your applications: early application deadlines before in early November, most typically with a decision by the end December (known called Early Decision) and regular application deadlines before February with a decision by May (called Regular Decision). Early Decision applications are binding, which means if the applicant is accepted by the college, he must attend that college.

You might be wondering why a student would want to commit to a college so early in the process. The answer is that colleges are increasingly reliant on maintaining high yield rates (that is, ensuring that a high percentage of students they admit actually end up enrolling), so Early Decision gives them an easy outlet to admit students with the assurance that they won't end up matriculating somewhere else.

In addition, many universities (either in lieu of or in addition to the Early Decision option) offer an Early Action option. Early Action is similar to Early Decision, allowing the applicant to apply early and obtaining an admission decision early, but the decision is not binding.

There are some private universities that have restricted (or single choice) Early Action, meaning that a student is not allowed to apply Early Action to any other private universities, and therefore can only take advantage of public colleges' Early Action options. For the most part, however, students should plan on applying via Early Action to multiple colleges, but Early Decision to only one.

☞ TIP 81: *Apply early with rolling admissions*

Some schools offer a pathway for entry known as rolling admissions, which basically means that they accept students as they apply, rather than waiting until a specific date to notify applicants of their decisions. In some cases, this might mean that if you apply early in the fall, you can hear back within weeks regarding your admission. Because schools that employ rolling admissions fill up their entering class as students apply, it is advisable to apply as early in the fall as you can.

Most schools that utilize rolling admissions are on the less competitive side, and many don't even accept recommendation letters or essays, so you can apply early without having to prepare some of the materials that other schools later on will require. Even if a school that uses rolling admission isn't your top choice, having an acceptance letter under your belt early on in senior year can give you boost in confidence as you go about applying for more competitive schools with deadlines later in the fall or winter.

☞ TIP 82: *Understand the benefits of Early Decision*

There are a number of surveys and trend analyses on the web showing that applying early to colleges can improve the chances of acceptance. One good source for these statistics is U.S. News & World Report.

The difference in acceptance rate between an Early

Decision applicant and a Regular Decision varies across colleges, but for some colleges, applying early could boost the acceptance chances by up to 20 percent! Note the following table that shows the undergraduate admission statistics for some top colleges for the Class of 2023. As you will notice, the difference between the percentage of admitted students in Early Decision and Regular Decision pools is quite substantial for many universities.

College	ED pool	ED accepted	ED %	RD pool	RD accepted	RD %	Total pool	Total accepted	Total accepted %
Brown University	4230	769	18.18%	34444	1782	5.17%	38674	2551	6.60%
Harvard University (SCEA)	6958	935	13.43%	36372	1015	2.79%	43330	1950	4.50%
Northwestern University	4399	1073	25.00%	36180	2319	6.40%	40579	3392	8.90%
Duke University	4839	880	18.19%	36761	2101	5.71%	41600	2981	7.17%
Cornell University	6159	1395	22.60%	42841	3788	8.84%	49000	5288	10.60%
University of Pennsylvania	7110	1279	17.99%	37850	2066	5.46%	44960	3345	7.44%
Columbia University	4461	650	14.57%	38108	1540	4.04%	42569	2190	5.14%
Johns Hopkins University	2068	641	31.00%	30163	2309	6.71%	32231	2950	9.15%

Compared to the Class of 2022's numbers, the landscape is even more competitive for the most part:

College	ED pool	ED accepted	ED %	RD pool	RD accepted	RD %	Total pool	Total accepted	Total accepted %
Brown University	3502	738	21.07%	31936	1828	5.70%	35438	2566	7.24%
Harvard University (SCEA)	6630	964	14.54%	36119	998	2.80%	42749	1962	4.59%
Northwestern University	4058	1073	26.44%	36367	2319	6.40%	40425	3392	8.39%
Duke University	4090	875	21.39%	33210	2123	6.40%	37300	2998	8.04%
Cornell University	6319	1533	24.26%	44681	3755	8.40%	51000	5288	10.37%
University of Pennsylvania	7074	1312	18.55%	37408	2419	6.50%	44482	3731	8.39%
Columbia University	4085	650	15.91%	36118	1564	4.30%	40203	2214	5.51%
Johns Hopkins University	2037	610	29.95%	27091	2284	8.40%	29128	2894	9.94%

Deciding on what colleges to choose for which category is one of the most important decisions that you will have to make during this process. Applying Early Decision is not a decision to be taken lightly, but it can be a major boost to your chances of studying at the school you've always dreamed of entering.

☞ TIP 83: Take advantage of Early Decision II

There are some colleges that offer Early Decision II, which tends to have application deadlines that run concurrent to Regular Decision deadlines. Like Early Decision, this is a binding option, but is a great avenue for students to take a second bite at the apple, so to speak, when it comes to improving their overall chances at a particular school.

The same benefits that come with Early Decision apply for Early Decision II, but with the extra information that comes from seeing how successful the first round of Early Decision and Early Action schools went, can enable you to more strategically target a particular school that might have caught your interest later in the process.

☞ *TIP 84: Make the right choice for Early Decision and stick to it*

The importance of applying strategically is best illustrated with a real story of a brilliant student who had been a consistently excellent performer and achiever across the board. Based on his profile and interests and a lot of planning, he narrowed down his dream college choice to a college that was highly selective, but was not in the Ivy League. During the application process, he somehow got persuaded by his parents and other family members that he should consider applying Early Decision to one of the Ivy League colleges, as some of his peers were also applying to those colleges, and the prestige associated with these schools was a strong lure.

Unfortunately, he did not get accepted into his Ivy League choice, even with Early Decision. Once he found out that he was not accepted at the Ivy League school, he applied to his original top choice college as a Regular Decision applicant, and unfortunately, he did not get accepted there either.

All his hard work and planning to attend a college that he really wanted to enter was squandered due to his last minute switch to a school for which he had not sufficiently demonstrated interest beyond the Early Decision commitment. And when he reverted back to the school for which he had demonstrated interest in more varied ways, it was too late, and not being part of the Early Decision pool meant he could no longer show the school just how personally committed he actually had been.

We hear these stories from students and parents all the time, and sometimes it's too late to reverse the consequences of careless decision-making. However, you can avoid this type of unfortunate outcome by being more deliberate in your choices.

☞ *TIP 85: Devote the extra effort for honors programs*

At some colleges and universities, admission into honors programs are out of your hands, and are based on some combination of GPA and standardized test scores that automatically place you in the running to be invited to join the school's honors program. In some cases, however, admission into honors programs is not automatic, and you must choose at the time you apply whether or not you want to be considered for admission into a school's honors program. In this situation, the most common next step is that you will be asked to write one or more essays in addition to the personal essay and any supplemental essays a school requires.

These essays can often be quite substantial, though, and ask you more than just about why are you interested in the honors program. Therefore, even if you don't think you necessarily qualify for entry into a school's honors program, you should apply anyway, especially if it means having an additional essay or two to expand on your academic strengths or otherwise communicate something about yourself that you could not address in the required essays. Admissions will read every essay you submit, so it's always better to give them more, not less, to work with as they get to know you better.

☞ *TIP 86: Don't panic if things don't go perfectly*

What should you do if you are deferred or waitlisted from your top school? First of all, the most important thing to understand is that these outcomes do not mean "Rejected." This simply means that the college does not have enough information at that time to admit immediately and would like more of it. For example, they may have seen a sudden dip in a student's grades or a borderline standardized test score, which would signal to a prospective candidate that a retake might be in order.

They might also just be waiting to see what the larger pool of applicants will look like in the regular decision round (and beyond in the case of a waitlist). It's key that a student not sit back and just wait. There are still a number of things you can do to advocate for yourself and your qualifications for a particular school.

☞ *TIP 87: Maintain your high standards, and aim even higher*

The first, and most important, step you can take to demonstrate your commitment to a school is to demonstrate your commitment to yourself. This means maintaining your grades and your extracurricular activities, and challenging yourself to perform even better than you already have.

Beyond maintaining your existing credentials, however, you can also re-take any standardized tests for schools that will still accept them before their regular decision deadlines.

☞ *TIP 88: Be persistent with your schools*

You should also keep the school informed regarding your continued growth, such as any updates on your academic or extracurricular record. Below, for example, is an example of a letter of continued interest that helped a student ultimately be admitted after receiving a waitlist decision.

"Dear [NAME OMITTED],

It's been almost four months since I first submitted my application. However, I'd like to provide an update because a lot has happened in my life since then.

In mid-March I received the exciting news that I had received two awards from the [NAME OMITTED]. In addition to this, I have been invited to speak about my research. This is particularly exciting for me as this serves as a culmination of six months worth of research, involving meticulous planning, experimentation, and data analysis.

Outside of the lab, I've also achieved new milestones. In terms of debate, my partner and I recently qualified for the [NAME OMITTED]. I have also recently qualified for the Tournament of Champions in Public Forum. In addition, our forensics team has opened up the annual spring session of our middle school outreach program, so I am currently fulfilling my obligations running the debate program.

Lastly, I had worked with several of my friends on a project that we have recently launched. Our project, called [NAME OMITTED], is designed to connect students of all backgrounds with tutors in order to further their education. Whether learners and teachers seek voluntary or paid learning experiences, it offers services to meet its users' demands. Through this resource, users can locate not only free tutoring services through local high schools but also paid-services from experienced and established tutors. As of today, this program has already matched dozens of students with tutors.

To conclude, I wish to address the question that every single admissions department always asks of their applicants: Why our school? At yours, one thing stood out to me above all others: the culture. I might not be admitted just yet, but being a part of the school's Facebook page, I believe, is a microcosm of that. Its incredibly funny pictures, ranging from an obsession with bagpipes setups to a comparison of Hershey's chocolate and entropy, highlight the one-of-a-kind environment I want to experience as an undergraduate and what makes your community my first choice. Ultimately, the question that I believe ought to be asked is: What makes our school unique? And the answer is simple... everything. Thank you for your continued consideration."

STEP TEN RECAP:

Once you have chosen which colleges you will be applying to, consider strategies such as Early Decision or Early Action that will help maximize your chances of admission.

If you are deferred or waitlisted from a college, you can still maintain communication with the school to help yourself stand out as it continues evaluating you for potential admission.

ADDENDUM

Planning for Funding College

MYTH: I can't pursue aid if I don't qualify for federal assistance.

What exactly is financial aid? It seems like a pretty basic question that should invite an equally basic answer. Despite this, many driven and passionate students remain stuck in a cloud of confusion, overwhelmed in a sea of options.

There are indeed many factors underlying a considered and effective financial aid strategy, but there are some worthwhile tips to note to help simplify things.

☞ *TIP 89: Know that financial aid can take many forms*

Simply defined, financial aid is money to pay for college. It is typically either given to students as grants that do not need to be paid back, or loans that help a student attend a college or university. It can come from a wide variety of sources, including the federal government, schools themselves, and privately funded organizations.

Different forms of aid operate in unique ways. However, the overall process of obtaining aid can be quite straightforward once you have devised a clear plan for doing so.

☞ *TIP 90: Work out the logistics of your aid strategy*

Before seeking financial aid, you want to have a clear sense of what kind of college or university institution you'll be attending, along with where it's located. Knowing your specific area of study is also helpful for private scholarships in particular.

If you are concerned about your ability to fund college, your college selection and financial aid strategies should run parallel to each other. Why? Because where you ultimately enroll may rely on the particular kind of aid that is available—not just from the school, but from other sources as well.

Each school (and in some cases, individual academic programs within a school) vary in total costs. Therefore, it's advisable to figure out what all the options you're considering will add up to in terms tuition, room and board, travel, and other expenses. This will give you a good estimate of how much aid you should pursue in order to cover as much of these expenses as possible.

☞ *TIP 91: Look beyond a school's price tag*

Be aware that even though a particular school might seem prohibitively expensive at first glance, you can explore opportunities to obtain financial aid that could mitigate the sticker shock and put that school in the running with schools with much lower tuition on paper.

If you're willing to put the time in to pursue private scholarships in particular, you will find a wealth of opportunities for thousands of dollars in grants, so don't let a school's tuition costs alone close the door!

☞ *TIP 92: Research the specific requirements for your aid*

Each and every grant, scholarship, loan, or any other form of aid is accompanied by its own specific set of eligibility requirements. And so, based on what you applying for, you may first need to fulfill financial aid requirements such as demonstrated financial need, a minimum GPA, in-state residency, a commitment to study a particular major, a certain gender or ethnic identity, or specific achievements in areas like athletics or the arts.

Make sure you research this beforehand so that you don't waste time on scholarships for which you're not actually eligible.

☞ TIP 93: *You might not qualify, but apply anyway*

An important note: it's always a good idea to apply for financial aid even if you're not sure that you qualify. Tragically, a high number of grants and scholarships remain unclaimed because families don't pay close enough attention to the criteria for eligibility, or, assuming a scholarship was more competitive than it actually is, simply did not feel it was worthwhile to try.

Another major reason to pursue aid in all its forms is that the majority schools are categorized as "need-blind," meaning that applying for aid will not have any negative impact on your admission odds.

☞ TIP 94: *Compare offers*

When you are been notified of your admissions decision by a school, you will also be given your expected family contribution, along with the combination of loan, grant, and/or work study aid that comprise the school's financial aid package. Because each school calculates these figures differently, though, you can use this to your.

You have the option to share with a school that there is a gap in aid between its aid package and that of another school that has already accepted you. At their discretion, they may adjust their financial aid package accordingly, especially if you can clearly convey how this gap might prevent you from being able to enroll.

It is indeed sometimes the case that a family's ability to afford a school is contingent on even small amounts of additional aid, so it's a good idea to compare offers. Schools want to do everything they can to ensure that the highest possible number of students they have accepted ultimately enroll, so you would be wise to take advantage of this option for your Regular Decision schools.

Early Decision candidates, of course, have much less wiggle room to compare offers. After all, they've already committed to the school.

☞ *TIP 95: Seek out resources for additional funding*

There are a wealth of outside resources you can use to obtain merit scholarship aid from both federal and private sources. Websites such as eScholarships.org, Fastweb.com, and IEFA.org offer hundreds of potential opportunities for aid.

Final Thoughts

IMPORTANCE OF PARENTS' INVOLVEMENT AND CONTRIBUTION

Parents can play a very important role in helping their children reach their goals. In fact, this book is designed for parents as much as it is for students. As with any new and unfamiliar endeavor, children need help navigating the college admissions process, and while we're delighted to offer our expert advice, the best coach for your child is you. You can't just hand this book over and expect them to know exactly what they should be doing with it.

With that in mind, here are some ways to make your active involvement in your child's college admissions journey as healthy and productive as possible.

☞ *TIP 96: Be a constant source of motivation*

The college admission process is the most stressful and strenuous activity that a student goes through, both mentally (and physically even!). The volume of tasks to take care of can pile up significantly, even before senior year hits, and many students just get burned out. It's very important for parents to understand what their children are going through and make sure they spend time with their children – listening to them, being supportive, motivating them and showing that they are there for them always.

☞ *TIP 97: Know when to back off*

While it's important to be your child's most enthusiastic cheerleader, sometimes all they want from you is an escape from the stress of college admissions. Don't put a damper on their enthusiasm for this process by constantly bringing it up in moments it might best be left alone, and don't turn dinner into yet another lecture about what your child still has to do, hasn't gotten around to, or might consider doing. Even in a process as involved as college admissions, balance is key!

☞ *TIP 98: Don't compare or criticize*

Parents talk, and inevitably, discussion can turn to what their children are doing, what colleges they are applying to, and what acceptances they may have already received. Don't let the whirlwind of chatter take you off course or, even worse, compel you to start comparing your child to other students or criticize them for not doing what their peers might be doing. Ultimately, each college admissions journey is different, and the moment you stray off your ideal path is the moment that might just sabotage everything you've worked so hard for thus far.

☞ *TIP 99: Share experiences*

At the same time, though, other families can also be an invaluable resource. Whether you are in contact with parents who have already gone through the process or ones just starting out, there is much to learn from both ends, and you can benefit meaningfully from being open about the goals you and your child have established. After all, maybe that parent neighborhood group or online discussion forum will suggest the perfect activity you haven't considered, or provide a nugget of wisdom that can propel you forward in your plans.

CHARTING YOUR NEXT STEP

There is a myriad of information out there, fragmented and spread out across an infinite expanse of sources. From the start, our goal was to create a centralized guide that could capture the entire college admissions process in a uniquely comprehensive way. Above all, though, we wanted to provide an invaluable resource that could help entire communities. To this end, we at Everest College Prep have pledged to donate a percentage of this book's revenue to charities committed to providing greater access to educational opportunities for underprivileged students and families. We humbly request that if you have found our advice helpful, to please share this book with other families who might also benefit from it.

Our Ten Steps and the associated actionable tips can serve as the framework for charting the course that will, at each turn, give you the confidence to know that you're making the right decisions. Indeed, each of the Ten Steps we have outlined is a project of its own, a significant undertaking that requires deep consideration, deliberate thought, and concerted collaboration. So what is next?

By reading this book, you have already taken an incredibly important step toward achieving your admissions goals. However, it's only the beginning. We know that every family is unique, with its own specific needs and concerns that no book, no matter how all-encompassing, can perfectly address. If you have any questions, you can visit us at **www.everestcollegeprep.com** to learn more about the Ten Steps. There, you can also schedule a free initial consultation to help discover the plan that best fits you. Together, we can make your journey a profoundly successful one.

The main takeaway?

☞ *TIP 100: Take the leap into your college admissions success story.*

INDEX

ABOUT THE AUTHORS

JONATHAN EVANS

 Jonathan Evans is the CEO of Everest College Prep. He has worked as a private college admissions consultant for seven years, providing guidance to over 500 students and families. Under his guidance, students have gone on to attend prestigious universities such as Harvard, Princeton, Stanford, and all of the top 25 colleges as ranked by the U.S. News & World Report list of top U.S. universities. As regional representative of Essex and Morris County's Princeton University alumni network, Jonathan regularly conducts college interviews with prospective students. He worked as a consultant for the Newark-based Research and Development Council of New Jersey, where he provided insights into how schools and communities can work together to provide greater opportunity for underserved, low-income students seeking college experience. Jonathan taught at Princeton High School and Madison High School, where he developed strong working relationships with families and developed a keen sense of families' unique concerns regarding the college admissions process.

ABOUT THE AUTHORS

BHASKAR SAMBASIVAN

Bhaskar Sambasivan is currently working as the President and Chief Strategy Officer at a Life Sciences services company focused on the commercialization of medicines and devices and improving patient experience and quality of life. Bhaskar has been working in the Life Sciences industry for more than 25 years and was recognized by PharmaVOICE group as one of the most 100 influential and inspirational leaders in the Life Sciences industry in both 2017 and 2018. Bhaskar is passionate about bringing access to education and information to all students regardless of their economic backgrounds, and has been an active sponsor of programs that help provide academic enrichment to underprivileged children around the world. Bhaskar has worked with many students and their families to mentor and help them get the most out of their high school and college experiences.

Made in United States
Orlando, FL
29 December 2021

12646945R00082